The
Power
of Association:

Success

Through Volunteerism and Positive Associations

By Henry E. Ford
Author of *Success Is You*

KENDALL/HUNT PUBLISHING COMPANY
4050 Westmark Drive   Dubuque, Iowa 52002

*"The more you surround yourself
with the presence of greatness,
the more difficult and unreasonable
it becomes to fail. "*

Henry Ford
From **_Success Is You_**

Ford & Associates
P.O. Box 393
Twinsburg, OH 44087-0393
(216) 425-8776

Note: Area Code Change to 330 is being considered

Printed in the United States of America
10 9 8 7 6 5 4 3 2 1

Cover Design by
Henry Ford

Foreword by
Dr. Robert L. Lawson
Author of *Destined For Greatness* and *Oh Yes We Can!*
Speaker, trainer, mentor and
Director of Continuing Education, Shawnee State University

Edited by
Jean L. Ford
Vice President, Human Resources
College of Art and Design - Pasadena, California

Associate Editors
Semara *"Sam"* Burton & Tabitha *"T.K."* Burton
Students in the Twinsburg, Ohio City School System

When others doubt, you must believe.
When others give up, you must start up.
When others let go, you must hold on.
When others laugh, you must smile.
When others are at the end of their
knowledge, patience and endurance,
you must call upon . . .
The Power of Association.

Henry Ford

Quotes

On Learning. . .

"Nothing could be more tragic than for men to live in these revolutionary times and fail to achieve the new attitudes and new mental outlooks that the new situation demands."

Dr. Martin Luther King, Jr. - **_Where Do We Go From Here: Chaos or Community?_** (199)

"The challenge is to focus on your dreams, goals, and objectives while simultaneously remaining open and flexible to new ideas for improvement."

Lucius Lewis - **_A Better Way of Taking Care Of You_** (8-3)

On Synergy. . .

"It catalyzes, unifies and unleashes the greatest powers within people."

Stephen Covey - **_7 Principles of Highly Effective Leadership_** (263)

On Volunteerism. . .

". . .There is no sustained success in a vacuum."

George Fraser - **_Success Runs In Our Race_** (130)

"Become the hub, not a spoke. I knew how the game worked. I knew one thing, it's easy to get rid of a spoke, but if you take the hub away, you don't have a wheel."

Harvey Alston - **_Be The Best_** (73-74)

Dedication

Dedicated especially to my mother and father who provided the foundation and the framework for the life that I seek to lead.

Dedicated to other family and friends who have had such a profound impact on my life by the way they lived their lives.

Dedicated to those who have taught me to reach higher in search of excellence. Dedicated to those who have taught me to stoop lower to help another human being.

"Once people have experienced real synergy, they are never quite the same again. "

Stephen Covey
7 Habits of Highly Effective People

CONTENTS

Foreword

"The Power of Association, as Victor Hugo would say, is an idea whose time has come." Through his words and experiences, Mr. Ford, a prolific and revealing writer illustrates and demonstrates in a clear, concise and succinct fashion what a significantly powerful impact other positive people can have upon each other when they take the time to interact.

This book is most beneficial to the reader in that it shares common sense knowledge and sensible approaches that others can use to enhance their business base in a practical manner. The concepts and ideas discussed in this book can apply to one's personal life as well.

I have watched my own speaking and writing career blossom and develop as a result of many of the concepts and ideas that Henry Ford talks about putting into place. The concept of networking is a powerful subpoint of the association process. For example, when Henry and I started working together and building a trust relationship, it became easier for us to recommend each others materials to other people.

When I first met Brenda Watkins at an Ohio Speakers Forum meeting, she introduced herself and in the same breath asked if she could purchase $120.00 worth of my books. What amazed me was that I didn't even know that she knew that I had written a book. It turns out that Henry Ford had told her all about it. Brenda was eager to find out more.

One of the things that I have learned in life is that people don't buy your products; they buy you. If your character matches the work you are producing, people sense that genuineness and they buy your product. Through this book, Henry Ford will introduce you to many organizations, many personalities and many ideas that you can put to work immediately in an effort to help you move to the next level of success in your life.

What's most exciting about the book is that the characters are not fictitious. These are real events, real stories and real people combined with substantive, practical ideas and strategies that subscribe to the fascinating and effective power of association. Just as he did in his first book, _Success Is You_, Henry has expanded his philosophy to demonstrate how, once you reach a certain level and get yourself into a position to help others, then you can begin to utilize the multiplier effect and put yourself in high gear as success becomes us. I find it interesting that the letter "us" can be found in success, Don't You? Hmmmmmm!!!

Dr. Robert L. Lawson

Preface

My very strong belief in the power of association is present throughout my speeches and writings. Without the power of association, I would have no story to tell. Without the power of association, each of us would remain a prisoner of yesterday. We would have no stimulus to affect positive change, and no belief that we needed to change.

Without the power of association, our talents, our knowledge, our limitations, our vision, our preconceived notions and our prejudices would be frozen in time. We would be denied the very human characteristic of personal development.

Without the power of association, I would not have the informative, powerful, diverse talents of my associates in the section entitled *Contributing Writers*. It is through them and other positive and supportive individuals that I have been able to bring myself from the debilitating depths of negativism to the lofty heights of enlightenment and empowerment.

If I am truly a product of my environment, then it is to my associates that I owe a debt of gratitude. Despite the title of my first book, *__Success Is You__*, and my belief in personal accountability, I acknowledge the undeniable fact that success and greatness is all of us.

Each of us can be educated, encouraged, motivated, challenged, cautioned, protected, inspired, restrained and promoted by all the others. We are the synergistic result of a multitude of people and circumstances. Always endeavor to make the wise choice in your associations, and your light will shine with the energy of one of the world's greatest and most infinite resources, *The Power of Association*.

Acknowledgements

Thanks to God for allowing me to wake up of sound mind and body and have available the infinite resources of others. Thanks to everyone I acknowledged in *Success Is You*. . .and more.

Thanks again to my wife *Dianne*, my sister *Jean*, my brother *Aaron* and his wife *Lela*. Thanks to the *'old'* friends and acquaintances, and to the new.

Thanks to *Sherryl, Tabitha "T.K."* and *Semara "Sam" Burton* for reviewing parts of this book. Thanks to *Ralph Burton* for always being so encouraging and supportive.

Thanks to *Shirley Craft* for your continual support and for reviewing this book. Thanks to you, *Larry Craft* and *Eloise Johnson-Rhodes* for attending the program in Sandusky.

Thanks to *Bert & Willie Gardner* for being there no matter what the need, no matter what the hour. I could write a book on the two of you.

Thanks to *Mrs. Leatha Little* on Craven Avenue for raising such a beautiful family and for telling all of them how much she enjoyed *Ready For Takeoff*.

Thanks to *Ben and Betty Suber* for purchasing so many copies of *Success Is You*. Thanks for continuing to promote, support and refer me to others.

Thanks to *Harry and Mary Sykes* for continuing to promote, support and refer me to others.

Thanks to *Karen Watanabe*, postal service representative, for helping us prepare an important mailing.

Thanks to everyone who has supported me. Thank you for your prayers, for your wisdom, for your understanding. Thank you for believing that I would like to list each one of you by name, but the list is too long, and it grows daily.

Thanks for teaching me that the road to success is truly lined with well wishers, the number of which defies quantitative measurement. Thanks for teaching me that along that road are people of competence, character and commitment, the value of which defies analysis.

Thanks for the foundation and the belief that caused me to write this book. It was not scientific theory, it was not a magical prophecy, it was not fictional writings, but it was *YOU* who proved *The Power of Association*.

Take that proof, along with personal conviction, power and purpose, and go forth into the world believing that you are capable. Develop habits that cause you to act in accordance with that belief. Decide that you can find *A Better Way of Taking Care of You*. To those who may doubt you, show them that despite them trying to inflict upon you *Peculiar Pain*, that *One Monkey Don't Stop No Show*. Demonstrate to yourself and the world that with *The Triumph of The Spirit* and *The Power of Association*, you can *Be The Best*, that *Success Is You*, and that you are *Destined For Greatness*.

Introduction

In the beginning there was Adam and Eve. And what we have been taught about the apple should impress upon us **The Power of Association**. Common wisdom would tell us that Adam thought he was in charge, yet he did not hesitate to claim *"That woman made me do it."*

And such is life today, we think we are in charge, yet we are influenced by our associations. So the question becomes, shouldn't we be as selective as possible about those associations? Shouldn't we be involved with those who might enhance our being?

We came into this world lacking the ability to survive without a powerful association with another, yet we did not choose that association. We came into this world needing the knowledge, experience and concern of others. Yet too often we try to *'go it alone.'*

We came into this world in many colors and different genders, prejudged and associated by stereotypical definitions, yet we did not choose our color or gender.

We came into this world exposed to different values, some placing the concern of others on par with their own, and some giving them no place at all. We did not choose those values.

We came into this world on different rungs of the economic ladder, some learning poverty of material things from the dictionary, and others knowing it as a constant companion. We did not choose our place on the ladder.

It is the *circumstances of life* which established where we began, and that falls into the category of *History*. It is the *gift of life* that gave us the *possibilities*, and that I would call *Amazing Grace,* It is the *toil of life* that will give us the *probabilities*, and that I refer to as *A Matter of Choice,* Are you reliving *History,* second guessing *Amazing Grace* or working on your *Choices?*

If everyone could sing a beautiful song, there would be no one to enjoy the music, no one to give a standing ovation, because everyone would be singing. What you may perceive as your weakness is simply an introduction to someone else's strength.

What is different among us keeps us weak only if we remain divided. Those differences make us even stronger if we are united.

Each of us has a God-given right and a responsibility to be the most we can, with what we have, right now! This book is about using the power and purpose of your being to plant, nourish and cultivate the seeds of greatness, so that all might enjoy a bountiful harvest.

This book is about bringing your main dish to the table, so that the resulting banquet can feed and nourish the hearts and minds of all.

This book is about doing in spite of, doing with the assistance of, doing in conjunction with. It is about exchanging the discomfort of stagnation and individual limitations for the experience of growth through positive relationships.

This book is about CHOICES. May yours be prudent and productive as you experience *The Power of Association*.

- SECTION ONE -

REALIZATION, JUSTIFICATION AND IMPLEMENTATION

I Didn't Know That I Didn't Know

Can It Be, Is This Me?

No Place For Ego: Don't Get Bad Getting Good

The Mechanics of Association

Informal Associations

Formal Associations

The Players

Perceptions

Chipping Away At The Glass Ceiling

You Are Competent, But It May Be A Secret

Find A Comfortable Fit

"Out of the melting pot of less than perfect individuals can come finished products, services and ideas that more closely resemble the maximum of human potential."

I Didn't Know That I Didn't Know

When I wrote *Success Is You*, I devoted an entire section to the importance of relationships to the process of success. I thought that would be enough, but it wasn't. *Success Is You* became available just nine months prior to my beginning this book, and I'm just beginning to understand what I thought I already understood.

I now have nine additional months of networking with individuals committed to personal and professional growth. I now have nine additional months of networking with individuals who are determined to make a difference, nine more months of people who don't say they can't, but ask how soon.

What a Difference a Day Makes, a popular song, but a very underestimated concept. *Twenty-four little hours.* How meaningless the minutes and hours seem to us. We often hear that the longest journey begins with a single step, yet how often have we not started a project or process because the *'finish line'* seemed so far away?

I cannot choose any twenty-four hour period during the past nine months that has been the most important. Some days pass without my recognizing that I did anything significant. Yet the results of the past nine months speak for themselves. *Success Is You* has sold over 40% of the first printing. I have enjoyed an over 400% increase in speaking engagements. I have been a guest on a radio talk show, and been invited to return.

I've received the public endorsement of two of America's best known speakers, writers and businessmen, Les Brown and George Fraser. I am associated with leaders in the field of motivation, leaders like Cassie Adams-Lewis, Horace Bey, SeMia Bray, Patricia Wingard Carson, Angela Craft, Maurice Curlee, Dr. Robert Lawson, Lucius Lewis, Aleta Mays and Ilinda Reese. I've had the pleasure of appearing on the same program as noted author and speaker Harvey Alston, and had the opportunity to learn from him.

Yet it all took place one step at a time, a pace many people feel is too slow. Yet I ask the question, how else do you get from point A to point B? No man nor creature I am aware of travels any other way than one step at a time. So let us begin.

Can It Be, Is This Me?

So what is this magic transformation that has occurred during the past nine months, a transformation second only to birth? You might even consider it a birth, the birth of a dream. I've done nothing spectacular. I've just done what I urge others to do, learn and share and commit and persist.

What, you ask, has made the difference? I'll tell. When you bring your best to the table, and acknowledge that you want to be even better, and commit time and energy to your goals, unforeseen, unseen and powerful forces begin to work in your behalf.

People and circumstances begin to create a very strong support system, one that you probably could not have envisioned or put into place. That support system increases your probability for success. As the old Chinese proverb states, *"When the student is ready, the teacher will appear."*

The difference is that you don't hear *can't* as much as you hear *can*. You don't hear *won't* as much as you hear *will*. You hear *it's possible* more often than you hear *it's not possible*.

When you improve your associations, your knowledge base becomes the combined wisdom of you and your associates. You increase your capacity to deal with adversity, because your choice of options now includes the combined experience of you and your associates. Your energy level and commitment increase because you cannot keep up with the thinkers unless you're thinking, and you cannot keep up with the doers unless you're doing.

Because of the diversity of heredity, gender, environment, training and aspirations, a healthy mix of ideas and ideals create soul searching moments that invoke the power of synergism. As attitudes are questioned and aptitudes peak, weak ideas are strengthened and strong ones reinforced. Out of the melting pot of less than perfect individuals can come finished products, services and ideas that more closely resemble the maximum of human potential.

As you increase your positive associations, your negative associations are automatically reduced, just because of the limitations of time. In this instance, the reality of only twenty-four hours in a day becomes a plus rather than a minus. You no longer have time for the dumb stuff!

As you increase your positive associations, people begin to treat you differently. Some offer you more respect and consideration and support, because they recognize a rational, focused, unstoppable individual.

Others, in jealous denial, begin to avoid you. Don't be overly concerned when that happens. It might well be God's way of removing negative forces from your life without you having to do anything at all. Good riddance to those who sought your company simply for their own greedy purposes, and are not willing to accept the new you.

No Place For Ego: Don't Get Bad Getting Good

I must interject words of caution at this point. If you are on the correct path, new associations will not create in you an inflated ego. There is a difference between believing that you're *as good* as anyone else, and believing that you *are better* than someone else. Each of us puts on our pants or dress the same way. Each of us has weaknesses and flaws.

Part of what makes us special is taking frequent and large doses of humility and understanding. As you grow in strength, grow in your capacity to understand the weak. As you grow in knowledge, grow in your ability to understand ignorance. As you go up the ladder, reach down and pull up. The bad fortune of others, as well as your good fortune, might well be temporary as well as illusionary.

The Mechanics of Association

You might be asking, how does this power of association begin? Do you go sit in the library and wait for someone to come along who looks studious? Do you begin your conversation with *"I want to become a new person by associating with you?"* NO.

The mechanics of association should not be mechanical. Informal associations are like those associations we might recall from our childhood. My mother warned me about being in bad company, hanging with the wrong crowd. *"If they do something wrong and go to jail, you'll go with them, whether you did anything or not,"* she would warn.

I took the hint, or rather the order, and spent my adolescent and teen years with those who stayed on the right side of the law. In those early years it was difficult, maybe impossible to tell who was going to be successful, but it was generally those who stayed far from trouble.

As I look at those who have become excellent examples, I see individuals such as Norman Thomas, a co-founder of RAN Associates in Cleveland.   I see William (Pepper) Boyd of Boyd's Funeral Home.   I see Richard Newsome, a former educator.   I see Kenneth Cloud, doing the sometimes thankless but always important job of juvenile rehabilitation.   I see Judith El-Amin, using charm and wisdom and tact to raise students closer to their maximum potential.   She worked tirelessly for years with INROADS.

I think of Dr. Rodney Foster, who is now a very successful and respected dentist and businessman.   Powerful, strong and fast, he could have focused only on sports in school, but had the vision and the wisdom to strengthen his mind as well as his body.   He and his wife Wanda are among the most powerful role models in their community, complementing each other by their business savvy, goals and aspirations.   They set examples of excellence by their personal and professional standards, each one standing on the shoulders of the other.   A perfect example of *The Power of Association*.

Informal Associations

Taking my mother's advice was the first step on my journey to positive associations.   Throughout our lives, we are faced with decisions relating to these informal associations.   Expounding on the pros and cons and other considerations of informal associations would be rehashing what most of us already know. You are judged by the company you keep, and later in this book, I'll discuss more about how perceptions are responsible for doors that open and doors that close.

All of us are products or byproducts of informal associations. Informal associations are not optional, except for those of us who are hermits. We have little choice but to be exposed to the good and the bad of informal associations.

Formal Associations

My purpose in this book is to share some thoughts about formal associations. I define formal associations as those associations that you make a conscious, deliberate effort to become involved in. During my lifetime, I have been involved in many. Some of these associations are civic, some social, some professional. Some are informal and loosely structured, while others bear a haunting resemblance to a rigid corporate structure.

The purpose of this book is not to evaluate these associations, but to share with you how they have the potential of adding value to your success index. In ways more numerous than you or I might imagine, the best training available for improved competence and commitment will be found in formal associations.

The Players

Sharing the information about formal associations requires that I share some of my experiences. It requires that I offer a diverse menu of organizations that have contributed to my growth.

The organizations I have selected include the *Black Data Processing Associates*, the *Ford-Bryson, Hansie Solomon Family Reunion*, the *National Association of Investors Corporation (NAIC)*, *The Chicago Eleven*, *The Dream Team* and *Worth Sharing Communications*, among others.

If you haven't heard of any of these organizations, don't feel like the Lone Ranger, most people haven't heard of them. Part of the beauty of organizational dynamics is that there are powerful, competent, committed, successful people all over these United States and the world, just waiting to share their secrets of success. The positive attributes I've just listed are available in countless organizations, everywhere.

A common thread that ties together the organizations I've listed is that they are volunteer organizations. *"OH, NO" you shout, "I knew there was a catch, I ain't volunteering for nuttin' honey."*

STOP, don't put this book back on the shelf, don't resign yourself to a life of stunted growth because you're afraid that you might give more than you receive. Volunteer organizations are the most effective, economical and practical training arenas available.

You can take Dale Carnegie courses until your wallet looks like a pancake and your credit card statement looks like the national debt. You can attend seminars seven days and nights a week. You can spend a lifetime studying in the classroom. You can do all of the above. No matter what you do, the reality is that one day you will have to take what you know and become involved. You will have to take what you know and actually do something.

Why not do that something in a volunteer organization and hone your skills during the process. The experience you gain cannot be purchased, begged, borrowed or stolen, and neither can the contacts.

Perception

There is much to be said for maximizing who you are through wise and effective marketing. Perception is important, but so is substance. I am reminded of a famous quote of Winston Churchill that was so eloquently used by Dr. Martin Luther King, Jr. that *"Truth crushed to the earth shall rise again."*

As a speaker and writer, the words and thoughts I share need to be based on firmly grounded values that can withstand the scrutiny of others and the test of time. My book *Success Is You* needed to be powerful and memorable, so that I would feel comfortable putting my real name on the front of this book.

"It's not what you know, it's who you know." What a demoralizing belief if you happen not to know anyone. I insist that it is both WHAT and WHO you know. As my speaking career has grown, I've had the occasion to try many methods of marketing myself. I won't even attempt to count the ways. Most of them work sometimes with some people.

I had the good fortune twice during the first six months of 1995 to have both Les Brown and George Fraser stand in front of audiences ranging from seventy-five to over eight-hundred, and say positive things about me. To those of you who may not know, both Les and George have an extensive list of accomplishments that speak for themselves. Trust me when I say they are popular and powerful, and that is more than perception.

You would not believe the rush of excitement I experienced as people scrambled to find out more about me, all because of a few words from Les or George. So it appears that it might be who you know.

BUT WAIT, what about when the excitement subsides and I have to speak, to respond, to negotiate. What happens when my battery is not connected to the high voltage, electric personality of Les Brown?   What happens when I have to operate off my own power?   Is my battery an Energizer or Brand X?   What happens when Les leaves for his next engagement and George starts signing autographs and selling books, and I'm left all alone, with WHAT I know?

My point is that you need both substance and support. First of all, credible people are not going to stand in front of an audience of several hundred and say good things about you unless they believe in you. So the accolades you get from them, you will probably have to earn.

The second point is that you are not going to survive off those accolades very long. You have to keep doing what you do, in fact, you've got to get even better, because now you've been labelled as good and you are in the spotlight. Now you are subject to the additional scrutiny that goes with increased recognition.   You cannot be on stage without being in the spotlight, and you cannot be in the spotlight without being under the microscope.   Quentin Smith in *Marketing: A Look At The Real Intangible* tells us *"Packaging lasts only as long as your potential customer doesn't 'pull the covers back' to take a hard look at the product (197 Bemley, 1989)."*

So perception is important, but it is not a gift. You are likely as the Bible says, to reap what you sow. When you plant your seeds, as you cultivate your crop, be sure to employ *The Power of Association*. Let those who have already reaped a bountiful harvest know who you are and what you do. Don't be afraid that promoting them will hurt you. Regardless of what you're selling, the supply of excellence cannot keep up with the demand.   *The Power of Association* is available, it is empowering, it is rewarding, it is necessary.

Chipping Away At The Glass Ceiling

One of the world's best kept secrets is about the learning that takes place beyond the walls of our educational system. Another of those secrets is about the networking for employment opportunties that takes place outside the Human Resource Department, where hiring and promotion decisions are supposed to be made or affected. There is a wealth of information, contacts and possibilities within volunteer organizations.

For minorities, there are additional considerations and benefits. Often, the lack of close contact with high level staff and management hinders our forward progress. It is much easier in business and social circles for high profile individuals to surround themselves with those who look, act and think like they do. That is a normal human tendency. It is also a significant barrier to the upward mobility of African Americans, women and other minorities. What *The Power of Association* allows and encourages is the opportunity to network with those who often are unavailable in a more structured business or social environment. Breaking down the barriers of misunderstanding is a natural result of *The Power of Association*. and you ultimately can be the winner.

It's a lot easier to *'show your stuff'* when you do it because you love it and you're good at it. Eventually, the money will come. As you continue reading, you will find examples where I stepped into a position of responsibility within a volunteer organization and exceeded the minimum daily requirements of the position. In that process, I sometimes learned from others, sometimes shared knowledge with others, sometimes I just *'connected,'* but usually I did all of the above.

The net result was that I had the opportunity to learn what I otherwise would not have learned, share what I otherwise would not have shared, and meet who I otherwise would not have met.

You Are Competent,
But It May Be A Secret

What was perhaps most beneficial was that I began to realize that I was competent. Learning that fact alone encourages and energizes one to go beyond predefined limits that have been established, often by others, sometimes by you.

Predefined limits are established for a variety of reasons including the jealously of others, cultural deprivation and ignorance.

The old school of employer-employee relations can be a major detriment to you creating and maintaining a strong personal belief system. In that scenario, you have to fight to prove you can, while part of the employer wants you to not be very good, for fear that you might expect to be rewarded with higher pay or more respect.

The irrational but persistent fear is that everyone is better off operating under the MDR philosophy. The MDR or Minimum Daily Requirement philosophy encourages the employee to do just enough to keep from getting fired, and encourages the employer to treat the employee just well enough so he or she won't quit.

There is little that is more empowering than finding out that you weren't the worst class that ever graduated; that you aren't the nerd your ex-girlfriend called you; that you are in fact a contributing member of society.

I reasoned that if I could develop a membership manual for BDPA, that I could develop procedures that benefitted business. I reasoned that if I could market the services of NAIC, that I could market for FORD & Associates.

In some cases, organizations I was involved in consisted primarily of people at a socio-economic level that would have made it unlikely that we would have even met. In other cases, these individuals occupied positions within the corporate world that would have made our meeting unlikely.

Let me caution you against attempting the shortcut of joining an organization for the sole purpose of meeting someone influential. Influential individuals are seldom naive, and you're not likely to succeed with *"Good Morning Mr. Smith, I'd like a free crash course on how to become a millionaire."* In organizations as in life you reap what you sow, and in the mean time and in between time, you feed and nurture and cultivate.

Find A Comfortable Fit

Your best chance to become happy and successful through organizational involvement is to become involved in something that is of interest to you. If your only source of satisfaction comes from what you expect to get, organizational involvement is not for you. The good news is that with the wide range of organizations already in place and needing serious minded individuals, certainly somewhere there has been prepared a place for you.

Another option is to start your own *'Help The Whatever.'* Like-minded people will be drawn to you because you are doing what you enjoy and it will be reflected in the way you relate to others. No one wants to volunteer to be around unhappy and unmotivated grouchy individuals. Those are the individuals you are probably trying to escape from. Whatever you decide to do, make sure that it makes you happy first, then watch it help make you successful.

- SECTION TWO -

READY FOR TAKEOFF

The Challenge, The Speech, The Results

"Your challenge is to get them (the students) from 0 to 60 in less than five minutes."

Beverly Bell
Cuyahoga Community College

*"Whatever your vision,
whatever your goals,
try to put yourself
in the position of
the people you serve."*

The Challenge, The Speech, The Results

In my first major speaking engagement in the Cleveland area, my challenge was to deliver the Alumni Address to the 1991 graduating class of Cuyahoga Community College, also known as TRI-C. I had graduated from TRI-C about seventeen years earlier, earning both an Associate In Arts and Associate In Science.

I was considered as a possible speaker based on an article that appeared in the Twinsburg, Ohio *Bulletin*, the community newspaper that serves the area where I currently reside. That was another example of possibilities brought about because of my involvement in community service.

I was contacted by Beverly Bell, a very personable young woman who informed me that my challenge would be to address the graduates with something motivational and memorable, without taking a long time to do it. She informed me that I needed to *"get them from 0 to 60 in less than five minutes."*

Although the maximum allotted time was five minutes, the speech had major implications for me. At that time, I was virtually unknown as a speaker. As a lifelong resident of Cleveland and its surrounding suburbs and cities, most of the people I knew had the potential for either being at TRI-C during my speech, reading about it in a newspaper, or hearing about it from friends or relatives.

My entire and very new speaking career hinged on less than three hundred seconds. Three hundred seconds of comments to an audience of graduates, guests, educational and community leaders expected to number 6000 people. Three hundred seconds of comments to students, parents, other relatives and friends who wanted to get it over with and celebrate.

Three hundred seconds of *'just words'* following the student speaker, Tyrone Morgan, a Summa Cum Laude graduate, who ranked first in a class of 2053 students. Three hundred seconds of *'just words'* preceding the keynote speaker, the popular Congresswoman Mary Rose Oakar.

Failure was not an option. Not doing it was not an option. In the words of Les Brown, *"Leap and the net will appear."* But don't leap blindly I thought, prepare for landing and use a parachute.

I knew the speech needed to be meaningful, memorable, powerful and unique. As I began to formulate ideas, I realized that it would make the person who hired me happy if I kept her challenge in mind as I spoke. So if I could satisfy my first customer, that would only leave 5999 to go.

I realized that everyone who would be at Public Hall for the program would have to feel needed and appreciated if my speech was to be a success. As I visualized myself in the role of everyone I could imagine that would be at the graduation, I could honestly feel good about what was developing.

Since the TRI-C speech, in every speech I've prepared, I've attempted to put myself in the place of the audience. Whatever your vision, whatever your goals, try to put yourself in the position of the people you serve. If you do that, I honestly believe you will enjoy the success I am enjoying. . .and more.

Today I still meet people who recall hearing that speech and often they ask if I will share a copy. One of the greatest tributes that can be paid to an individual is to be acknowledged in such a positive way.

So based on popular demand, please disconnect your telephone and doorbell, send the family to McDonald's, find a comfortable chair and join me as I share *Ready For Takeoff.*

Good Evening,

It is a great honor to be with you tonight.

It is an honor because I am among students who are realizing their hopes of a brighter tomorrow.

It is an honor because I am among parents who have sacrificed so that their children can seek and attain goals higher than anyone ever imagined.

It is an honor because I am among husbands and wives, brothers and sisters, sons and daughters, who have absorbed extra duties, critiqued assignments, and in other ways assisted the graduating students.

It is an honor because everyone in this auditorium shares in some way the dreams of everyone else.

When I was asked about speaking before you, I was told that the challenge was to get you excited about your future, to get you from 0 to 60 in less than five minutes.

The fastest way I know to travel is by jet aircraft, so I decided to visit the airport. When I arrived, there was a conversation beginning between a TRI-C graduate and the Control Tower. We all know that the Control Tower is that higher power in our life.

Anyway, the conversation I heard went something like this.

Control Tower to Graduate, please listen to the following instructions carefully.

In your mind, you may think you cannot fly. But ALWAYS remember the story from the first grade, The Little Engine That Could.

The runway is dark. As a TRI-C graduate, rather than curse the darkness, you are expected to light a candle.

On your right hand side is your TRI-C Diploma. It is your Pilot's License. Understand that it will take you as high and as far as you wish to go.

Understand that in order to become the most that it is within you to be, your vision must be more than 20/20. You must see the future not as it is, but as it can be.

To your left is your flight plan. Study it well, because it will set your direction.

YOU are the control panel.

Common sense and experience is your radar. Use them to avoid life's hazards.

Love and compassion for your fellow man is your temperature gauge. Don't let that temperature drop too low.

In your bombsights you will see poverty and discrimination and disease, and other forms of human suffering. Use your arsenal of knowledge and patience and understanding to help rid the world of these destructive elements.

Your fuel gauge registers one-half tank. The one-half is education and background. Understand that the tank is half-full, not half-empty. You may refuel while in flight with more education, and with a positive attitude and persistence.

Congratulations graduate, you are now prepared for takeoff.

Graduate to Control Tower, Graduate to Control Tower, but how high shall I fly, and what is my destination?

Control Tower to Graduate, Please listen carefully, this is the conclusion of our transmission. Remember that your attitude determines your altitude. I suggest that you fasten your safety belt, set your sights upward, open your throttle wide, and aim for the moon, for even if you miss, you'll land among the stars.

The audience went absolutely wild.   When the applause subsided, Interim TRI-C President Ron Sobel took the microphone and responded to me *"Mr. Ford, they will not soon forget you,"* and then he asked them to applaud again. And they did!

The Keynote Speaker, Congresswoman Oakar took the microphone, turned around to me and replied, *"I don't know why they needed me to speak."*

As I was leaving TRI-C, the chairman of TRI-C's Board of Trustees, the late Owen Heggs, stopped his car, blocked traffic and let down his car window to congratulate me.

The TRI-C newspaper, the *Intercom* reprinted much of the speech. Accolades came from Beverly Bell, the commencement committee and several adminstrative staff members at the college.

So I put TRI-C in perspective and thanked God that I did as well as I did, while realizing that I'm only as good as my last speech. Don't ever rest on your laurels, for that which has brought you to this point, cannot take you where you want to go.

- SECTION THREE -

THE BLACK DATA PROCESSING ASSOCIATES:
GROWING THROUGH PROFESSIONAL ASSOCIATION

"With each mile and every new passenger/member, the train changed a small amount. At every station/chapter new ideas, enthusiasm, and commitment joined the train."

From *Get On Board* by Vivian Wilson
Former National President, BDPA
(1 *Data News*, Summer, 1990)

"Because of the associations he formed, because of the challenges he undertook, because there was a BDPA, today this individual is making a living doing that which the aptitude tests and society told him he could not do."

Growing Through Professional Association

I am reminded of a true story of two young African American men from Philadelphia; Earl Pace Jr. and David Wimberly.

These two young men, well educated and proficient in the field then known as data processing, had wisdom and vision beyond the technical requirements of the computer. They understood that hidden within the opportunities of the 1970's, were the pitfalls of racism and sexism.

They understood that the power and potential of the computer was so awesome that African Americans needed to become more educated and dedicated, but also needed a network of others who shared common challenges and possibilities.

They understood that those who took for granted the seemingly open arms of corporate America were bound to one day wake up and find that America had returned to business as usual.

They understood that like anything else that was good, it could not be assumed that minorities would be adequately represented.

They understood the concept of what was later to be called synergism, the concept that one plus one equals more than two. They understood the motherwit that tells us two heads are better than one, that united we stand, divided we fall, and that there is strength in numbers.

So these two young men formed an organization called the Black Data Processing Associates, better known as BDPA. Looking back beyond the wisdom of experience, many would think it foolish that two young African Americans could begin a movement that would mobilize a people and revolutionize an industry.

Today BDPA is a forty-seven chapter national organization. The member benefits include local and national newsletters, information exchange meetings, an electronic bulletin board, professional development opportunities, workforce development, cultural diversity, public awareness and extensive community service.

Beyond the stated benefits lie those opportunities limited only by the imaginative minds of BDPA members nationwide.

So what is my point? Why did I choose to bring you this story? The reality is that visionary young men saw in the mid 1970's what is today revolutionary to many. They saw the necessity of association, they saw *The Power of Association*.

Here is another story. It is the story of a young African American who worked in the data processing field for fourteen years before finding out about BDPA. This young man worked in an organization that offered decent pay and benefits. The soothing effects of *'just enough to get by'* gave this young man the crippling disease of complacency.

Locked out of major decision making positions, this young man spent years working beneath his potential. Despite having a good job, this individual was not in the *'good old boy'* network. The mechanism for growth and achievement was just beyond the glass ceiling.

In 1986, this individual joined the Cleveland, Ohio chapter of BDPA and soon after became membership chairperson. Through the organizational challenges, and with the inspiration and help of other African American professionals, this young man grew in character and wisdom, becoming a credible asset to the organization.

In 1987, this individual was named Member of The Year of the Cleveland Chapter of BDPA and nominated for national Member of The Year. In 1988, at a BDPA national conference, this individual first heard Les Brown. At other national conferences, he heard Joshua Smith and a host of other successful people.

Because of the associations he formed, because of the challenges he undertook, because there was a BDPA, today that individual is making a living doing that which the aptitude tests and society told him he could not do. That individual is the author of the book you have in your hands, and much of my success, I owe to my participation in the Black Data Processing Associates and to *The Power of Association.*

I felt strongly enough about the BDPA experience, that I co-sponsored a member of the Cleveland Chapter's Computer Competition Team. That team went to Philadephia in August, 1995 and went through the process of learning, sharing, competing, networking and associating with other positive teens. While I was writing this book, I received a thank you letter from Aliesha Younger, a young lady who was an alternate on that team. That thank you energized and empowered me. I was the giver, but then suddenly I became the receiver.

Aliesha, I don't know you and don't know how to reach you, but hopefully someone who knows you and reads this book will give you this message. You are competent and considerate. You have the power and purpose to go beyond the limited vision others may try to burden you with. Continue to seek positive situations and positive people, and you and those around you will continue to be winners through *The Power of Association.*

According to Phillip J. Stella, *"One excellent platform for networking is professional groups and associations (25 **Cose Update**)."*

- SECTION FOUR -

THE FAMILY REUNION EXPERIENCE

Recollections by Henry Ford

Reflections by Beverly King

"Many have left the red hills of Georgia, and other places in the South, but let us thank God for their humble beginnings, because we could not be today what we are, if it had not been for them."

From *Reflections* by Beverly King

*"They thought we were
the rich and famous.
Only we knew that we were
the broke and the busted.
But we were special
at that moment because of
The Power of Association."*

Recollections by Henry Ford

Perhaps the most challenging group of individuals to work with is family. Operating under the banner of love and shielded by the protective proclamation that *'blood is thicker than water,'* family offers opportunities that you should expect nowhere else. The bad news is that the banner and the proclamation can and often are used to defy imagination, create stagnation and avoid great expectations.

Trying to get family to function in a business-like and effective manner is often met with super critical remarks and bad feelings that can last a lifetime.   The family is unique in that its members had little choice about who the other members would be.

Their interests, aptitudes and attitudes are as diverse as one could imagine.   And the prevailing comment when faced with challenge is that *"If you loved me, you wouldn't have said that,"* or the belief that *"You have to accept me, we're family."* Being related is elevated to having supremacy over logic, reason and fairness.

In spite of the challenges that working with family can present, we've done it anyway.   For twenty-two consecutive years, a chapter of the FORD-BRYSON, HANSIE SOLOMON reunion has given a family reunion.   Has the planning ever been easy? NO!   Has the reunion always been fun? YES!   Have the relationships been inspiring, productive, rewarding and character building?   To me they have, and on the next few pages I'll explain some of the reasons why.

I hope within these pages will come the inspiration for you to begin or increase your involvement in family reunions, for you will find that they truly offer you *acres of diamonds*.

Our family reunion began with a dream in the early 1970's. My late cousin, Synnia Solomon worked toward making the reunion a reality. It was her premature death before the first reunion plans were finalized that brought together family members in Cleveland, Ohio. In her memory, it was decided that the reunion plans must go forth.

So we joined together and had the first reunion in Cleveland in 1974. That year and since then there have been disagreements about dues, hotel sites, menus, participation, fundraisers, the name of the reunion, the name of the chapter and whether we should serve potato chips at the picnic because of the relationship of salt to high blood pressure. But through it all, we have met and become better acquainted with relatives all over the country.

My speaking career began and was enhanced because of the family reunion and people like Sherbia Jones and Ruth Mitchell, my second cousins whom I met at a reunion.

I have been inspired by young people in the family as a result of the Synnia Solomon Scholarship Fund that I started.

One example that comes to mind is Amanda Vinson, daughter of James *'Mann'* & Velma Vinson. Amanda was a top scorer on her high school basketball team and a high academic achiever.

I am reminded of some of the first scholarship winners, Bonita Pratt, Ardell Whitworth and Alfred Keith Littman.

Ardell, Alfred, their parents and Kindra Littman were featured in ***The Cleveland Reporter***. It was the first newspaper coverage of our reunion that I am aware of. The article also featured photos of Jean Louise Ford, Margaret Ford-Taylor, Lawrence Ford and Aaron and Lela Bryson.

From the creative side there is poet and author Arlene Jackson, co-author of *Make Time for This*, and author of *Ain't No Half-Steppin'*, *Howling Against The Wind* and *Champions of Change*. *Ain't No Half-Steppin'* is a book of poetry. *Howling Against The Wind* is a powerful fictional novel based upon the factual circumstances of illness and malpractice. *Champions of Change* is a book about ten famous African Americans.

There are those willing to plan fundraisers at places like Karamu Theatre, where we saw the Pulitzer prize-winning drama of *No Place to be Somebody* in June, 1974. We were exposed to a touch of class, in addition to a champagne sip after the show.

I recall the determination and controversy surrounding the decision to sponsor a reunion at Wheels Inn in Chatham, Ontario, Canada in 1985. I applaud the vision and commitment of that decision.

It was a decision that was highly criticized, particularly after Canadian authorities would not let the disc jockey into Canada to perform at the Saturday night affair. Small minds sprung into action with additional criticism, while visionaries found local entertainment, and most of us had a good time in spite of the circumstances. The incident challenged our fears, but it improved our adaptability and increased our knowledge base.

Then there are people like Bill Taylor, who with the necessary ingredients of calmness and confidence, avoided a possible confrontation with rowdy teenagers who attempted to intrude upon a reunion in Detroit. His unique combination of restraint and boldness diffused a potential problem.

Then there are people like Willa *'Tina'* Williams and Beatrice Andrews of Cincinnati, who sponsored a reunion for two-hundred people with the help of two friends. Along with

Mary Stallworth and Celestine Goodloe, they proved that *The Power of Association* was stronger than the challenges they faced. They planned and executed an excellent reunion, while larger chapters watched in amazement.

I can recall the commitment and flexibility of Willa Williams, Janet Nelson-Bali and members of the North Carolina Chapter as they joined together to sponsor the first reunion to take place in Macon, Georgia. They ignored the challenges of long distance planning in order to take the reunion back to *'our roots.'*

Then there was the support of Cleveland area community leaders like Beverly Anderson-Glover, Bertram Gardner, Jodie Goggans, Leonard Hardy, June Taylor and Betty Thomas who unselfishly devoted their time and expertise to the scholarship review board.

In 1984 my sister Jean Ford published her cookbook, *Sweet Potato Pie* and gave them as souvenirs at the reunion. She was able to accomplish this despite the fact that our mother had passed earlier that year.

We found corporate supporters for souvenirs that year from companies such as Van Dorn, American Family, Ohio Bell and NAIC.

Later years found us inspired by powerful and eloquent speakers such as Margaret Ford-Taylor and Barbara Williams. We graduated to celebrity status when Myra Coates and Leslie Davis shared the responsibility of presenting the scholarship awards.

Leslie rearranged her schedule to honor that commitment. She placed commitment ahead of convenience. Leslie was featured in *Ebony Magazine* that year and was named Miss Kentucky State. She is now Dr. Leslie Davis.

Celebrity status continued as Beverly Ford was acknowledged for being featured on the nationally aired **Barbara Walters Show**. The focus was on the generation we refer to as *"Twenty Something."*

Buffalo and the younger generation astounded the family when the Buffalo Chapter put it's Saturday night dinner and awards program into the hands of teens and preteens. The results were absolutely fantastic as the youthful Buffalo family members rose to the occasion.

Detroit took us on a trip down memory lane as they dug up records of parents, other relatives, family history and other pertinent facts. They displayed many antique items from the *"Old Home House"* in Georgia and from other places.

Dianne and I went to Washington, D.C. one year and ended up staying one block from the Holiday Inn where our cousin, Glenwood *'Tamp'* Williams operated his limousine service. Tamp chauffeured us all over Washington, and refused to take a cent for his troubles.

There is very little that compares to the stares of those who witness two African Americans dressed in blue jeans and t-shirts, getting out of a limousine to take pictures, and no one knows who they are. They thought we were the rich and famous. Only we knew that we were the broke and the busted. But we were special at that moment because of **The Power of Association**.

As I write these words, fresh in my memory is the 1995 reunion in Atlanta, Georgia. With just a few people scattered between Atlanta, Macon and Haddock, the Georgia Chapter did an excellent job, and attendance was up from previous years.

Peggy Martin, Ayanna Martin, Janice Temple, Mary Wallace, LaTasha Temple, Tanisha Moss, Lisa Jessie and Jeffrey Jessie provided a weekend of top quality entertainment. If I missed someone, I am truly sorry.

Missing from the reunion this year were Eddie and Marguerite Langston, who have been constant supporters of the reunions. They were always there with their video equipment recording the fun times. Marguerite became seriously ill early in 1995 and unfortunately passed away during the time I was completing this book. She is deeply missed, but the way she lived is an inspiration to us all. Our immediate challenge is to use *The Power of Association* to support and strengthen each other.

Many others who are no longer with us have greatly influenced our character. The lessons they taught are invaluable, the love they shared is irreplacable. We are better because they were in our lives.

The late Beverly King of Detroit worked very hard behind the scenes to keep the family newsletter and the scholarship fund going. She did much more, but these were two of my dreams that she helped me with. The last part of this section contains something Beverly wrote entitled *Reflections*.

I've tried to relate some of the people and circumstances that make a family reunion worth the effort. Unfortunately words cannot describe the feeling and facts do not adequately define the results of these past twenty-two years. For those of you impressed by numbers, let me share this with you.

Out of the forty-three individuals I have mentioned in this section, I didn't even know twenty-nine of them before we began the reunion in 1974. I cannot tell you how different my life would have been without the inspiration of these twenty-nine people. I can however assure you that I am a better person because of *The Power of Association*.

"Reflections"
from the Family
by Beverly King

To the family members of this great family. We, the Detroit Chapter of the Hansie-Solomon reunion organization greet you with love, in the name of Jesus. As we come together on this 20th celebration, we want you to reflect on some of the daily use of items and activities in a routine day.

Most of our homes were based on God and a family Bible was always there with records of important events and occasions within our family such as births, deaths and marriages.

A usual day would begin around four o'clock in the morning, with everyone up and "mama" would prepare breakfast, usually consisting of biscuits, salt pork, syrup and grits, maybe eggs. Our young family members went to the spring or to the well for water that was used with a dipper from the family pail. Some went out to take the cows to pasture, and to feed the chickens and tend to other animals on the farm. A day's work was almost completed by the time the children were ready for school, which was usually a one-room school building with several grades. School lunches were usually a syrup can with biscuits, salt pork and syrup. Reflect back with us on our colorful clothing, the humbleness that was usually exhibited in our daily lives. Everyone spoke to each other and we respected our elders.

Reflect again on some of the entertainment we enjoyed, the singing, reading poems, and dancing, even telling great stories in the evening.

We take great pride in our parents and our forefathers who took the time and sought to draw us together again, and to tighten the bonds of unity between us. We take pride in our young businessmen and entrepreneurs as they serve us and others in the community. We are proud of our Scholarship Committee and the things they have done for our youth.

We love you *"family members"* for taking the time to organize and make known to us, the family, the feeling of pride within ourselves and to be willing to challenge our lives today and its many opportunities.

As we walk down *"memory lane"* this weekend, let us try and feel their feelings of love, life and power.

Many have left the red hills of Georgia, and other places in the South, but let us thank God for their humble beginnings, because we could not be today what we are, if it had not been for them. So lets take part in this weekend, planned to commemorate *"Black Heritage,"* as we take a stroll down Memory Lane.

Beverly C. King - The Detroit Chapter (1993)

- SECTION FIVE -

THE NATIONAL ASSOCIATION OF INVESTORS CORPORATION

Structured For Learning

The Environment of Inclusion

The Regional and National Conferences

Affirmative Action In Investing

Support From A Chief Executive Officer

Awards and Rewards

"Get involved with organizations in the community that are going places and doing worthwhile programs. If you look at their resume, people that are successful belong to several organizations and give their time in service. Not only do they give, they get (73 Alston)."

Harvey Alston
Be The Best

"What corporate America often fails to realize, but NAIC was aware of, is that when you stay in 'your place,' so does your knowledge and your belief system."

My involvement in the National Association of Investors Corporation (NAIC) goes back to the mid 1970's, back to the time it was known as the National Association of Investors Clubs. Those who have read **_Success Is You_** and have great memories might recall a mention of NAIC. NAIC deserves much more than the few sentences that appeared in that book.

Although the publisher allowed me to go over my budgeted pages in **_Success Is You_**, I had so much that needed to be written, that I made the difficult decision to save the NAIC story until another time. Well, another time is here. I am sharing the NAIC story as it relates to personal and professional growth.

Structured For Learning

My involvement with NAIC began uneventfully, a result of me being inquisitive about the investment process. I can't even remember how I found out about the organization. I attended a meeting of the Northeast Ohio Council, the regional council of NAIC that serves the Cleveland-Akron area.

The business meeting of the council was open to the general public. It was a place you could go and watch, or even participate in the process. Based on the orderly process of the meeting I was convinced that I was on to something.

Missing completely from the meeting were references to *get rich quick* schemes. There were no people scampering around the room with *'a hot tip from their brother-in-law'* that required your total life savings and no questions asked. From the beginning, it was obvious that the organization was one of people focused on investment education, and that's what I was there for.

The Environment of Inclusion

I was extended an invitation to join the board of directors and I accepted that challenge. At the time I became a council director, I was the only African American on that board. In fact I was the only African American at most of the meetings. I am happy to report that the discrimination which has found its way into almost every area of my life was not apparent within NAIC. Whatever doubts, fears and prejudices that may have existed were not visible.

I quickly became publicity chairperson, and was soon immersed in a learning process that would change my life forever. Not only did I learn a great deal about the investment process, but also the communication process. There were many examples of how to go about finding, seeking and sharing information. Everyone was helpful, because they already knew what I was beginning to learn. They knew that the process of sharing information was one of the most effective ways to learn, to co-exist and to grow.

Missing was the backbiting and grandstanding that I found prevalent in corporate America. No one felt that what you learned might threaten their job. Destructive criticism rarely if ever reared it's ugly head, because it is unwise to abuse a volunteer. If conditions become bad enough, they can always leave because they can't pay their bills with the income from that position anyway.

Reflecting back, I realize that a major reason for the ideal learning environment was the diversity of the group. Even though I was the only African American on the board, there were businesspeople, company presidents, staff people, technicians, teachers, and others. In my entire working career, I never had occasion to sit and share information with such a diverse group.

In my experience, company politics, the pecking order and the protective policies of divide and conquer assure that you stay in *'your place.'* What corporate America often fails to realize, but NAIC was aware of, is that when you stay in *'your place,'* so does your knowledge and your belief system.

Reflecting briefly upon the last sentence, it becomes clear why we are a nation of so many separate agendas, with a growing disrespect for the rights and beliefs of others. Anyway, my challenge within NAIC was to grow and learn, and the regional and national conferences became my next goals.

The Regional and National Conferences

Every once in a great while, when you think you're beginning to know all there is to know, when you think you're becoming bored, when you think you've been as excited as you can become, there appears a regional or national conference.

There is a certain rejuvenating power that exists with a change of scenery, meeting new people and sharing in an even greater pool of knowledge. That rejuvenation is critical to your long term interest and effectiveness. I've attended several of those conferences and have never regretted my decision to attend.

Beyond the business of the conferences, the penetrating question that I asked myself was *"Where are the brothers and sisters?"* Where was the African American segment of the population? My experience at regional and national conferences was similar to my experience with the Northeast Ohio Council. There was always a feeling of warmth and a spirit of welcome wherever I went. Why then, was a segment of the population that so badly needed investment education always missing?

The percentages of African Americans in attendance ranged from as little as one percent all the way up to a startling four percent. I knew some of the answers to my question, but not all. But what I also knew was that I cared more about a solution than I did the problem. I was determined to try to do something about it.

Affirmative Action In Investing

I understood that the average income of African Americans was approximately 60% of their white counterparts, leaving them with less discretionary income. I understood that savings was taught at the dinner table in African American homes and investing was taught at the dinner table in the homes of White families.

It's only reasonable that you tend to do what you understand and are comfortable with. There was nothing I could do about the income disparity in the United States. A series of circumstances too large to understand and too painful to reflect upon continues to maintain that income disparity. I was having enough trouble dealing with the income disparity on my own job.

I did understand from my limited knowledge of investing that if saving money at the corner bank was possible, that investing was possible. I understood the reluctance of African Americans to step outside their comfort zone with their limited funds and step into the world of investing.

I also understood that African Americans purchased brand name products and luxury cars at a percentage level much greater than their sixty percent level of income. I understood therefore that a part of the issue was the choices that were being made.

I understood that major opportunities for growth existed in equity investing.   I knew from talking to other African Americans that a common belief existed that you need *A LOT* of money to begin an investment program.   I knew first hand from investing and reaping the rewards, that you *DID NOT* need a lot of money to begin an investment program.

I understood that many more Cadillac advertisements reached the African American community than did advertisements from Merrill Lynch.   I understood that investment education needed to reach into the African American community, even if it required a push.

The learning process I had involved myself in was quickly becoming a social issue.   I realized that simply recognizing the problem was not sufficient.   I was the one, self-appointed due to lack of any apparent leadership, to attack this issue.   If it was to be, it was up to me.

Having met and talked previously with Tom O'Hara and Ken Janke, chairman and president respectively of NAIC, I had no reservations about approaching them.   I proposed that NAIC embark on some type of drive to change the look of the investment community.   I wanted the investment community to look more like the community of consumers, somewhat in the range of fifteen to twenty percent African American. That meant heavy advertising directed toward the African American community.

Tom was well aware of my concern, but he also had the final responsibility for the cost effectiveness of NAIC's advertising and NAIC's financial viability.   I used the word BUT, and this is where leadership rises from the potential ashes of destruction.

Tom O'Hara had the perfect opportunity to take the easy wasy out, to not be bothered, to be insensitive to my concerns, but he didn't. He followed the advice of M. Scott Peck as he took *The Road Less Travelled*. He demonstrated innovative leadership by involving me in the solution of the problem I had recognized.

Tom agreed to send information packets to *"as many people as you give us names for."* He agreed to *'target market'* into the African American community. He agreed to spend time and effort to effect positive change, if I would stay involved in the process. And why wouldn't I, it was my idea?

Tom is a wise leader who realized that had he accepted the challenge as his own, and had I not been involved, he might have lost a contributing NAIC member and increased his own emotional, physical and monetary effort. The lesson here is that when you want to see change, be certain that you are willing to be a part of that change.

If I could give credit to any single effort for increasing my ability to write, it would be the letter writing campaign I undertook in pursuit of African American investing. I wrote to friends, associates, churches, schools, congressmen, African American organizations, *Ebony Magazine*, *Black Enterprise Magazine* and anyone else I could think of that could read.

I networked with the very few African Americans at NAIC conferences and strategized about how to go about bringing the benefits of equity investing into our communities. I spoke on occasion to interested groups including the Cleveland Chapter of the Black Data Processing Associates.

For ten years I kept the effort going, and just when I felt I was running out of steam, I was notified that I was to be awarded the prestigious Investment Education Award from NAIC. The truly astounding part of receiving the award was becoming aware of the identity of the other recipients. They were Lawrence Jones, chairman & CEO of Van Dorn Corporation,

John J. Phelan, Jr., chairman of The New York Stock Exchange, Martha R. Seger, governor of The Federal Reserve System and Louis M. Thompson, Jr., president of The National Investor Relations Institute.

Support From A Chief Executive Officer

Upon his return to Cleveland, Lawrence Jones was kind enough to send me a short letter. In that letter he congratulated me on my accomplishments and for the remarks I made at the conference. I was surprised to receive personal correspondence from a man who was the chief executive officer of a company the size of Van Dorn.

I responded with a note of my own, letting Mr. Jones know that I also enjoyed our meeting and looked forward to seeing him again. I expected that to be the last time I would hear from Lawrence Jones unless our paths crossed again as we went about our very different professional lives. I was pleasantly surprised the following spring to find Lawrence Jones passing out literature at the Spring Conference of the Northeast Ohio Council of NAIC. There he stood casually dressed, mixing and mingling well with people from all walks of life. Truly a gentleman and certainly an inspiration to those who seek to be judged by the content of their character and not by their station in life.

Would he remember me? Of course he wouldn't, the man meets thousands of people, he is busy, there are hundreds of people in here asking thousands of questions, and besides I've been told that we all look alike. As I approached, Lawrence extended his hand and said, *"Mr. Ford, how are you?"*

I can't really remember how I was, besides shocked. Anyway, between that time and when Lawrence Jones retired, we kept in touch, sharing occasional phone calls and notes.   On one occasion, Lawrence donated souvenirs for my family reunion. He truly seemed to appreciate my involvement in trying to share investment education with the millions of people who for the most part had never been *'in the ball game.'*

My relationship with Lawrence Jones proved that each of us can walk in the presence of greatness.   We just need to believe, persist, follow the path of positive thought and action, and remember *The Power of Association.*

The INVESTMENT EDUCATION INSTITUTE
of the
National Association of Investment Clubs
presents its

DISTINGUISHED SERVICE AWARD
IN INVESTMENT EDUCATION

---

to

Henry E. Ford

who as an individual learned early in his life how investment education could enlarge opportunities for the individual. With this knowledge and experience and a great concern for his fellow man, he has persisted against indifference and discouragement to persuade the media to recognize the merits of good investment education. His efforts have produced stories in national publications showing the value of sound procedures in selecting equity investments and the resulting opportunities afforded individual investors. He has thus aided the investment education of thousands of readers.

Geo. A. Nicholson Jr.
CHAIRMAN

Kenneth S. Janke
EDUCATIONAL DIRECTOR

The Power of Association, again showing just a little of the potential it carries.

Awards and Rewards

Receiving the award demonstrated that my efforts had not been in vain. I had believed, based on the lack of feedback from most people I contacted, that my efforts had only a minimal effect. What I wasn't aware of was that based on my efforts, **Black Enterprise Magazine** and NAIC Headquarters in Royal Oak, Michigan had begun a dialogue. I didn't hear from **Black Enterprise**, but they were hearing from and paying attention to me.

Those who have followed **Black Enterprise** over the past twenty years have probably noticed a growing emphasis toward articles about equity investing. I'll probably never know for certain, but I have to believe that I had an impact on that shift. That is the true joy of involvement, that is one of the benefits of *The Power of Association*.

I owe Tom O'Hara and NAIC's selection committee a debt of gratitude for acknowledging my efforts. They didn't have to do that, but often in life you get not what you want, but what you are. You get, in addition to what you expect, what others believe you deserve.

When you believe strongly enough in something, you must persist in spite of how you perceive the outcome. While others doubt, you must believe. When others give up, you must start up. When other let go, you must hold on. When others laugh, you must smile. When others are at the end of their knowledge, patience and endurance, you must call upon *The Power of Association*.

- SECTION SIX -

SPEAKER SUPPORT

The Les Brown Workshop

The Chicago Eleven

The Dream Team

Worth Sharing Communications

Toastmasters International

Other Pillars of Strength

*"Classes and training help with the skills,
however, alliances with influential people are
needed to further one's career (35 Bemley)."*

Marilyn Dyson,
Bonding For Excellence

"We were trained,
and inspired
and nurtured
and critiqued,
and then we would go
to the next step,
and start the process
over again. "

"I forgot that I scored in the lower twenty
percentile in persuasive ability.
I forgot that I had third degree stage fright
the first fifty years of my life.
I forgot that I didn't win
the speakoff competition.
I forgot that I couldn't do what I'm doing.
I forgot ALL of that,
but I remembered what I wrote to Les.
And I HAVEN'T changed my mind!"

The Les Brown Workshop

As part of my decision to pursue the dream of motivational speaking, I decided that I needed all the *'edge'* I could get. I didn't then, nor do I now consider myself what you would call a *'natural.'* I am however, persistent and committed. Things that I decide to do, I do with a passion.

Sometimes in early 1994 I received an advertisement from Les Brown Unlimited to attend one of several *Speaking For A Living* workshops. I had a choice of Chicago, New York or Los Angeles. The first workshop was scheduled for early June in Chicago.

I decided that if I was going to commit the time, effort and dollars, that I might as well get started. I'm glad that I committed early. The Chicago workshop not only exceeded my greatest expectations, but there were only sixty-nine in attendance, small by comparison to the next two workshops.

The attendees had almost three days of close contact quality time with Les, and each other. What was so inspiring about being in the presence of fellow speakers was the enthusiasm and fellowship. If you've never spent three days with sixty-nine highly motivated individuals, you owe it to yourself to do so, at your first opportunity, and most of the opportunities that follow.

Whatever your goals or your dreams, spend time around those with similar goals and dreams. What competition others will offer is insignificant in comparison to the knowledge, enthusiasm and growth you will experience.

One of the high points of the first evening for me was during the get-acquainted reception, when my wife Dianne met Les Brown. Les had already heard everyone speak briefly as we told something about ourselves.

No wallflower by any stretch of the imagination, Dianne introduced herself to Les. Les replied *"Oh, you're Henry's wife, I just love his voice."* Dianne responded like a professional when she said *"Well you work with him Mr. Motivator, 'cause I'M HUNGRY!"* Les knew then that I wasn't the only one in the family that listened to his tapes. More importantly, he knew that he wasn't the only one in the room concerned about my success.

Even though Les showed up early and stayed late for every session, we couldn't wait for him to start. We acted like we didn't need him, but we knew we did. People acted like they had known each other for years, and in most cases accepted responsibility for everyone else's achievements. Add Les Brown to the smoke we made and you can be assured we left there *'on fire.'* We were trained, and inspired and nurtured and critiqued, and then we would go to the next step, and start the process over again.

Les ended the last session on Saturday with such a powerful close that there were tears and sniffles from various parts of the room. With background music and special lighting effects, he challenged us to *"Be a bright light in an often dark world."* He cautioned us that probably only one, perhaps two of us would accept the challenge, even though he acknowledged that we all had the ability.

I later wrote to Les and told him that *"I was the one, that it was I who would accept the challenge."* When you are inspired by the greatness of those who have made it, and by the greatness of those who are on their way to making it, you will write and say and try anything.

I forgot that I scored in the lower twenty percentile in persuasive ability. I forgot that I had third degree stage fright the first fifty years of my life. I forgot that I didn't win the speakoff competition.   I forgot that I couldn't do what I'm doing.   I forgot ALL of that, but I remembered what I wrote to Les.   And I HAVEN'T changed my mind!

In the words of Dr. Leslie Davis, former *Miss Kentucky State*, *"two of the basic ingredients for success are a strong heart and a made up mind."*   Another important ingredient is to take frequent and strong doses of amnesia and apply them to the negative mental conditioning that keeps you from doing what you need to do, and keeps you from being who you have the potential to be.

FORGET THAT YOU CAN'T, AND YOU WILL EXPERIENCE THAT YOU CAN!

The Chicago Eleven

I was so inspired when I returned home that I wrote to all the other sixty-eight attendees.   I invited them to send me their biographical information if they were interested in a joint marketing effort.

Ten individuals responded, and for lack of a better name, I will call those ten and myself *The Chicago Eleven*.

I take this opportunity to introduce you to those people who not only showed up in Chicago and went through that process of self-improvement, but also went the extra mile.

The first one-sixth of a mile was believing that we could benefit from working with each other.   The second one-sixth of a mile was deciding to work with others.   The third one-sixth of a mile was planning to update and send the biographical information. The fourth one-sixth of a mile was updating and sending the information.   The fifth one-sixth of a mile was planning to send the changes and corrections. The last one-sixth of a mile was actually sending the changes and corrections.

If you want to win, you've got to *believe*, you've got to *decide*, you've got to *plan* and you've got to *execute*. Then you've got to go back to the drawing board and *redo* and *plan* and *execute*, and *keep on keeping on*!

Do not let the fact escape you that I, with no sales training and very little experience was able to sell fifteen percent of the attendees in Chicago on this joint project. Anyone in sales more than twenty-four hours knows that fifteen percent is not bad at all.

You don't grow or fail to grow based on what you are told. You grow or fail to grow based on what you BELIEVE and ACT UPON, or what you believe and FAIL to act upon!

Whatever your passion, you've got to believe it, and plan it, and do it, and redo it until it becomes second nature. Going the extra mile often causes your passion to become your reality. So here they are, the other members of *The Chicago Eleven*.

- Virginia Anderson Becker -

Virginia Anderson Becker, founder and president of Positive Pathways in Utica, Michigan.

Virginia is proof that dreams do come true. She met and married a loving, wonderful man later in life after much preparation. She shares insights and concrete action steps for achieving the dream of a loving, committed relationship through her workshops, seminars, and individual and group coaching sessions. Her teachings are founded in a spiritual belief system that works.

Virginia's background includes more than twenty-five years in education and training. She has a master's degree and an Educational Specialist Degree from Michigan State University and is a graduate of the Dale Carnegie program. Through her deep belief in an inner approach to making dreams become reality, she is now turning her teaching talents towards helping others learn this process.

- Sandra duMonde -

Sandra duMonde of Ann Arbor, Michigan, and president of Events duMonde can be described as innovative, talented and diverse. Her company's commitment to excellence is apparent as the current world tour coordinators for David and Gay Williamson, the authors of *Transformative Rituals - Celebrations for Personal Growth*.

Having the total responsibility for the logistics involved in such an extensive project has given Sandra invaluable experience in her field.

Busy authors can utilize the expertise of Events duMonde and focus on the primary requirements of their own business. Renewed energy and commitment discovered at the *Speaking For A Living* Workshop helped result in a new business for Sandra.

- Jay Leon -

Jay Leon of Effective Communications of Chicago, Illinois can answer the question, *"How can we teach young people responsibility while avoiding power struggles?"* Jay conducts lectures, workshops, seminars and consulting in how to develop responsible children.

With over twenty years of teaching experience, Jay Leon has also served the City of Chicago as a career counselor, the Chicago Public Library system as a trainer of tutors, and helped many people to communicate more powerfully, through his seminars and one-on-one coaching.

Jay uses his expertise to help you become more efficient and effective in helping children be responsible for themselves. He earned his Bachelor of Science in Education degree from Northern Illinois University, and is certified for and has experience teaching all grades in elementary and high school.

- Phil Nania -

One person that can truly *'set an audience on fire,'* is Phil Nania, trainer and president of Life Design Seminars in Somers Point, New Jersey. Phil is well known for the demonstration of THE FIREWALK. In the truest test of the power of the positive mind, Phil takes the audience far beyond rhetoric.

A severe stutterer when he began first grade, Mr. Nania was inappropriately diagnosed as learning disabled, failed to be promoted with his peers and subsequently became a behavioral problem. This set the stage for a long downward spiral for Mr. Nania which culminated in substance abuse and total loss of all his personal property and his dignity.

Having overcome these problems and gone on to achieve widespread recognition as a trainer speaks eloquently about his abilities.

After attending over 100 seminars over a fifteen year period, Phil developed his Power of Achievement Training. His training has been featured in televised and print media.

- David Nelson -

David Nelson of Wentzville, Missouri, is a writer and public speaker.   He has come a long way since divorce and bankruptcy.

David's background of twenty years in sales and six years of entrepreneurial experience, combined with the *Speaking For A Living* Workshop has created a *'sleeping giant.'*   David has dedicated his life to finding and working with people who want to make a positive difference in the lives of young and old.

David is the president of D.J. Nelson Seminars, a non-profit foundation whose purpose is to raise money to compensate young people who serve their community in a volunteer capacity and who dream of attending technical school or college.

David and a core group are currently working together to develop a seminar whose primary purpose will be to develop self-respect among teens through volunteer work.

- Leonard Pinkney -

Leonard Pinkney, Jr. of Chicago, Illinois is a high energy sales professional with a track record of achieving and exceeding established business objectives. He has extensive experience in creating highly profitable client relationships and negotiating win-win financial transactions.

Leonard's areas of proficiency include prospecting, probing and problem solving in technical environments, sales management, annual planning and personnel recruitment and training.

His decision to attend the *Speaking For A Living* Workshop added an additional level of refinement to a responsible and diverse background in business. Leonard has occupied responsible positions in a variety of well known companies including General Motors, IBM, Monsanto, Mays Chemical, Nutrasweet and the Central Intelligence Agency.

- Frances Pitt -

Some people just walk into a room and it becomes engulfed in a silence of awe. Frances Pitt is one of those rare individuals that you stop to listen to before she opens her mouth to say anything.

Frances is a resident of Milwaukee, Wisconsin. After she begins to speak, your attention becomes riveted to her every word. When she is half finished you sit there praying that she will continue for a long time. You just know that she will finish long before you are tired of listening. When she is finished, you realize that she is going to be a finalist in the speakoff competition at the Les Brown Brown *Speaking For A Living* Workshop.

Competence, personality, charm and warmth seem to be second nature to Frances. She keeps busy speaking and being involved in church activities.

- Zelda Robinson -

Chicago's own Zelda Robinson, the captivating voice of WJPC 106.3 FM is definitely a star on the rise. One needs only to listen to her voice mail message to understand why she is a favorite in the Chicago area.

In addition to providing Chicago area listeners with *Oldies Then and Now*, Zelda is a motivational speaker and also conducts workshops and seminars in group sessions and for individuals. Her *Pathways To Passion Brochure* summarizes how she turns dreams into reality.

Zelda's message focuses on helping people find their passion in life, and understanding how simple thoughts control their destiny. She teaches people how to alter the thought process to achieve desired results so they can live their dreams.

- Shela Sanders -

Quiet, reserved, caring, compassionate, respectful of others. Many words can be used to describe Shela Sanders of St. Louis, Missouri. So many, in fact, that you just decide after a few minutes with her that she is a quality person.

Always exhibiting excitement at other people's triumphs, Shela is truly the bright light that Les spoke of. Multi-talented but never overbearing, Shela's vast experience is in contrast to her youthful vigor.

Her employment background includes fourteen years of administrative experience which is put to good use in developing solutions to workplace challenges. Shela's experience with downsizing and outsourcing make her a particularly valuable resource in today's turbulent job market.

Her experience in serving the public is the basis of an unusually high level of understanding. She has the ability to motivate her audience before they even realize what happened.

- Rufus D. Stephens -

Rufus Stephens, a resident of Joliet, Illinois grew up as one of five children in a single parent home in Savannah, Georgia. He spent many of his formative years in rural Georgia with his mother who taught in a two room school building.

Rufus earned his B.S. degree at Savannah State College and pursued graduate studies at the University of Florida.

Rufus is an advocate for individual excellence. He speaks regularly to educational, church and civic organizations on subjects relating to personal and organizational excellence.

Rufus blends his resonant voice, his colorful speech and his warm humor in an unsually impressive fashion to move his audience from complacency to commitment and full appreciation of themselves.

The Dream Team and Worth Sharing Communications (WSC)

It is a common belief in life that those of us who have an idea, a product, a service, need to protect and defend it from those who don't. This belief is particularly prevalent in the African American community. The *'crab in the barrel mentality'* that has laid siege to the minds of otherwise rational individuals is the cause of much debate and probably just as much suffering.

I am happy to report that this commonly held belief is being successfully challenged. I'm not referring to a courtroom challenge, I'm not referring to eloquently written beliefs of those with fifty years of academic experience and zero years of real life. I'm not referring to fairy tales or soap operas.

I'm referring to the speaker support groups known as *The Dream Team* and *Worth Sharing Communications*. They quite possibly are the first two African American speaker support groups in the country. I am a member of both, and despite their uniqueness, they are so much alike that it makes sense to write about them in the same section.

The Dream Team . . .
Harvey Alston, Henry Ford, Dr. Robert L. Lawson, Aleta Mays, Patricia Wingard Carson

Shortly after joining the National Speakers Association (NSA) and Ohio Speakers Forum (OSF), I attended an OSF meeting where I met Dr. Robert Lawson (Bob as he prefers that I call him). As Bob and I talked, he shared a vision of networking and supporting each other and rising to the top together. Some things that sound too good to be true, are true nevertheless.

Although Bob resides in Huntington, West Virginia, his credibility as a speaker results in him travelling to many sections of the country to speak. Bob was contracted by Cuyahoga Community College in Cleveland to do a one day workshop entitled **Destined For Greatness.** Bob's workshop was scheduled for the middle of May, 1994.

I attended the workshop and in addition to receiving more than my money's worth from the workshop, Bob introduced me to Matt Krise of Kendall/Hunt Publishing Company. That was the beginning of _**Success Is You**_, and this book.

The following months brought rapid results as I met Aleta Mays, and Bob continued to use his influence to get us opportunities to speak. Almost fifty percent of my bookings during the first six months of 1995 were due either directly or indirectly to Bob's efforts. He truly is _walking the walk_ as well as _talking the talk_.

As unbelievable as it seems, just after I began this section, after working for several hours straight, I took a two hour break to pick up some cassettes, and do some other shopping. While I was away, Bob called and left a message asking me to tentatively block September 9th. He was working on getting five individuals onto a public television station in Detroit, to be followed by a book signing.

Before I could get back home to get the first message, Bob called back and left another message. We were scheduled for public television, a book signing and a possible radio spot. He wasn't working on Bob, he was working on us.

The way I met Aleta Mays was the way I've met many individuals through Bob Lawson, via mail and telephone. Bob has a habit of calling or writing and dropping the name of someone who is really moving toward their goals. He only does that if they appear to have the mindset to network with others.

He did that with Aleta and she and I shared information on the telephone and through the mail. The next thing I knew, Aleta was sharing my brochures, business cards, etc. all over southern Ohio, and SHE DIDN'T EVEN KNOW ME!

Based on conversation, aspirations and documentation, Aleta started selling me as a person. What better public relations can you have?   You cannot beg, borrow or steal that kind of promotion. Even if money didn't count, and I paid someone to do the same thing Aleta did, I would not have been inspired the way she inspired me. I ask you, is there any limit to *The Power of Association*?

Harvey Alston is another connection through Bob Lawson. It happened during one of those *'Columbus, Ohio'* weekends, where Bob, Aleta and I often converge for meetings of the Ohio Speakers Forum (OSF). Bob called me at the hotel to let me know he had arranged a meeting with Harvey Alston. At that time, Harvey was to me the mysterious photo in the OSF membership booklet that everyone was raving about.

Harvey's schedule is so packed that he has been referred to by a former president of NSA as *"the busiest speaker in the business, bar none."* I asked myself how Bob was able to arrange a meeting with someone of Harvey's stature, without a LARGE cash deposit.

It didn't matter, I met Bob at the appointed time in the hotel lobby. A few minutes later Harvey arrived, we introduced ourselves, we talked, and shortly afterwards, Aleta arrived.

Not only did Harvey meet with us, but he took us to his home in a beautiful suburb of Columbus. And what a home he took us to.   We met his wife, Toni and their two teenage sons, Paul and William. We were treated like royalty and I was in shock the entire night, and for a few weeks afterwards.

Harvey shared experiences, ideas, his *'system,'* his vision, and he asked us about ourselves. His office, covering the full length of his home, was loaded with awards, acknowledgments, books, tapes and everything else you might imagine from a speaker of his caliber.

During our ride to Harvey's home and back to the hotel he talked about the speaking business. He asked both Aleta and me how we would describe ourselves in thirty seconds. We shared ourselves with him in typical unrehearsed fashion.

Bob eventually spoke up and said *"Harvey, you didn't ask me to describe myself."* Harvey replied that he already knew what he needed to know. He replied that Bob asked *"Will you meet with US?"* not *"Will you meet with ME?"* Harvey continued, *"That told me all I needed to know."*

So that is another lesson in *The Power of Association*. A man whose time we could not have purchased, took the time and effort to help, because he believed that we were quality individuals.

Worth Sharing Communications . . .
Cassie Adams-Lewis, SeMia Bray, Horace D.S. Bey, Angela Craft, Maurice Curlee, Henry Ford, Lucius Lewis, and Ilinda Reese

As I've previously written, in June of 1994, I participated in a two and a half-day workshop developed and presented by Les Brown. It was entitled *Speaking For A Living*, and it was powerful. Les and others spoke of networking together and building a network of speakers to share a hope and a vision that many believe America has lost.

In late June, Les spoke at the Universal Truth Center in East Cleveland. It was after his speech that I met Lucius Lewis. Lucius attended the *Speaking For A Living* Workshop in New York City the following month. Until this point, no connection existed. The two events were unrelated, or at least I thought they were.

A few weeks later I received a letter from Lucius, inviting myself and other Cleveland area Les Brown seminar attendees to a meeting at his office. The purpose was to investigate the possibility of starting a speaker support group.

I attended, and *Worth Sharing Communications* was born. It didn't really happen all at once. We toiled with the name, the mission and the purpose. We knew the group needed to serve it membership and not simply exist for the purpose of existing, and it doesn't. Today, the eight members of *Worth Sharing Communications* have learned together, attended each others seminars, shared what works, shared what doesn't work, and empowered and encouraged each other to go beyond previously perceived limits.

One example of the support system is evident in the following paragraphs. My book, *Success Is You* was scheduled to be available on December 2, 1994. I received the first copies on November 30th and on December 1st I saw Lucius and he saw a copy of my book. Lucius had already planned a December 3rd book signing for his personal development series of *A Better Way of Taking Care of You*.

Lucius told me to bring some of my books to the book signing. I replied *"I can't bring my books to your book signing."* Lucius repeated *"Bring the books."* Lucius is over six foot, two inches, carries himself with the authority of (and somewhat resembles) Les Brown - and my wallet looked like a pancake! So what would I have argued about and why?

I sold seven books at someone else's book signing because he refused to be a *'crab in the barrel.'* That attitude has not been unique to December of 1994, nor has it been unique to the members of **Worth Sharing Communications**. Each of us is empowered by the others in a lesson on *The Power of Association* that is as convincing as any lesson you could receive.

The irony of **Worth Sharing Communications**, is that prior to meeting Lucius, his name was the one I heard most in the Cleveland area when someone would mention another speaker. He was the major local competition that I was aware of. Now he is the major local supporter, enhancing my career as I hope I enhance his.

Lucius, who was apparently the most firmly entrenched local speaker, was also the one that initiated the effort to combine forces. He recognized the potential of an expanded base of knowledge and inspiration. He recognized *The Power of Association.*

On July 20, 1995 members of Cleveland based **Worth Sharing Communications** and **The Dream Team**, with members in Ohio and West Virginia, joined forces to present a motivational seminar and book signing at the Hilton-South Hotel just outside Cleveland. Our power of association has just begun.

Toastmasters International

Many of us have heard of Toastmasters, and those who have never become involved are missing a golden opportunity for growth and *The Power of Association.* Toastmasters is an organization that provides solutions for one of the greatest fears on earth, the fear of public speaking. It has often been said and written that the fear of public speaking to many people is greater than the fear of death.

So what magic does Toastmasters provide that causes you to overcome this fear? There is no magic. Toastmasters is simply an organization committed to personal and professional growth, and dedicated to improving your communication skills.

Made up of individuals that have decided they don't want the fear of public speaking to interfere with their goals and their dreams. Made up of individuals that learn their fears are not unlike those of their neighbor, their co-worker or even their boss. Individuals that are willing to share with you what they have learned, and encourage you to share what you know.

According to well known and respected business consultant and writer Jeannemarie Caris-McManus, *"The only way in the world we can produce results is through other people - and communication is the essential skill (5 Cose Update)."*

One of the advantages Toastmasters has is that there are many clubs in all parts of the country and the world. You can't use inconvenience as an excuse not to belong to Toastmasters. If you do manage to find a remote location of the country that doesn't have a club, someone will help you form one.

Toastmaster members as a rule are highly competent by virtue of the process of continual self-improvement. My own experience with the Nordonia Gavaliers has been extremely positive, although I am not as active as I would like to be.

The pace of consulting, speaking, writing books, being an active member in two speaker support groups and the focused and intense training of the Ohio Speakers Forum and National Speakers Association has resulted in my missing most Toastmaster meetings. Someone from the Gavaliers periodically checks on me and reminds me that they would like to see me and have me share my experiences.

That is the kind of power of association that helps empower and encourage me.   I have more help available to me than I can possibly take advantage of.   If you are serious about overcoming the doubts and fears of public speaking, or simply want to improve your communication skills for personal or professional reasons, Toastmasters holds the key to your better future.

Other Pillars of Strength

Although Brenda Watkins and Ed Jones are not members of *The Dream Team* or *Worth Sharing Communications*, they deserve special mention. Both have been consistent supporters of our efforts.

Even though Ed lives less than eight miles from me, I met him through Bob Lawson at an Emancipation Celebration in Gallipolis, Ohio. Gallipolis is over two hundred miles from Cleveland, but I had to be there to make that connection. *The Power of Association* again flexes its muscle.

I met Brenda at an OSF meeting in Columbus. She recognized my name as that of someone who had recently talked with a co-worker, Tina Bates. It turned out that Tina was involved in doing an executive search, and had called me to help in that effort. The search was for an information systems professional, and Tina traced me through BDPA.   Again, *The Power of Association* was working.

Both Ed and Brenda have been to many of our seminars, purchased books and other products, referred others, and written notes and letters of encouragement. They have made themselves available in a variety of ways, without being asked.

Then there is Diane Swift. What do you do with a person who purchases *Success Is You*, reads half of it, puts the book down and calls to order fifteen more copies? You love and cherish her, that's what you do.

I've known Diane for many years and it has been a friendship of mutual respect. Easy-going, with a quick smile and a charming personality, Diane nevertheless floored me when she got that excited about what I was doing.

Nestled in the long-time friendships we think we know all about, is support that you could never dream of. Don't be afraid to share your hopes and your dreams with everyone you know. If you are as fortunate as I, there is a Diane Swift in your life also. *The Power of Association* is at work, even when the world is at rest.

Brenda, Ed and Diane are among those individuals that make our dreams possible. With that thought in mind, I feel comfortable making the executive decision of naming them as honorary members of *The Dream Team* and *Worth Sharing Communications*.

If there are any crabs in any barrels anywhere nearby, they certainly DO NOT show themselves in the presence of *The Dream Team* or *Worth Sharing Communications*.

- SECTION SEVEN -

SAVE OUR CHILDREN

"You also let us know that we are somebody and that we can be what we want to be and all that we can be."

Betty R. Scott,
Parent

In 1991 I received an *Achievement In Life Award* from the *Cleveland Plain Dealer*, Cleveland's daily newspaper. It was at that affair that I met a lady who referred me to Nancy Tondy. Nancy was in charge of coordinating a career day at the John D. Rockefeller Fundamental Education Center, which at the time was a magnet middle school in the Cleveland system.

My experience speaking at that school was so positive, that I have returned several years in succession. I have spoken at career days and a graduation. Since the restructuring of the Cleveland School System, John D. Rockefeller is now an elementary school. I will be returning there later this year to speak to some of the second graders in a pilot program that I have developed.

What made my experience there so positive? Why do I feel that I have 'adopted' a school? In addition to a responsive staff, it was the feedback from the students, the staff and also from a parent. You would be surprised to find that only one time during the years I have spoken within various school systems, have I received a written note from a parent thanking me for what I am doing. How often have I received letters from the students? Let me just state that the parents have very large task ahead of them if they ever expect to catch up with the students.
I have had parents come to me after an assembly and thank me verbally. I appreciate that, and I am sure that many others are thankful. As adults, we need to make sure that we go on record supporting that which we believe in. Opinion and positive reinforcement is what often drives the direction that individuals take in their relationship with others.

I received many letters and shared many greetings with these future leaders of tomorrow. The reward of a smile or an acknowledgment from these children who are growing up in such a troubled world gives me hope. If I inspire them half as much as they inspire me, then I have secured a reward that has eluded even kings and queens.   Young people today need to know that they are unique, that they are special, that they are cherished, that they are loved.   In return, they will often let us know that we are special also.   That too, is *The Power of Association.*

Some of the feedback I've received from children include comments like the one with the powerful message from Chisa Clark which said -

> *"I thank you for coming to our school to talk to us about responsibilities.   I know you probably had trouble on the way to our school, that's why I thank you so much."*

Chisa obviously associates getting to school with trouble. Perhaps trouble from bullies or from gangs.   As adults, we all need to be working on that problem.   Going to school should not require enrollment in *Basic Training 101.*

Nitasha Hearn wrote -

> *"Thank you for taking your time to come to our school and talk to us.   I think that the talk you gave us was very interesting.   Some people in this school really did need that talk. You know we're very sorry we didn't have enough money to pay you."*

Christina Jones shared these words with me -

> *"Your message was very strong, your message got me thinking about the future.   You are a very kind person to take your very own vacation time to speak to us.   The story about the control tower was a good success story. You are very generous to come and speak to us without getting a reward."*

Corika Lewis decided after hearing *The Entertainment Special* that she could *"Be like Vanessa Williams in **The Comfort Zone** or like M.C. Hammer - **Too Legit To Quit**, and like Mariah Carey she could **Make It Happen.** "*

A young man signed simply *"Your pal; Talon"* wrote *"I learned that you can do or be anything that you want.   Your speech really touched my heart and thank you again for coming. "*

Tiffany Wilson wrote -

> *"Thank you for sharing what you have to say to us. And coming to our school for a very nice speech to say to us. And get off of work just to come to our school you gave a very special presentation. "*

You can surely understand the connection I have formed with John D. Rockefeller.

During the past several years I have spoken at many other schools. Some of the more memorable include Shaw High in East Cleveland, Ohio, and Garfield Jr. and Garfield Sr. High in Garfield Heights, Ohio. It has always been an educational, challenging and rewarding experience.

The experience at Shaw High School could have been somewhat unnerving had I not realized that everyone is not ready for the message at the same time. As I entered the room into which two classes had been seated, about five students had their heads down on the desk, already prepared to *'ignore'* the message.

The coordinator who had arranged for me to speak, obviously embarrassed, explained that the fumes from the roof tarring that was being done had many students complaining of headaches or drowsiness. A very noble effort on her part, but when the bell rang after my presentation, there were no headaches nor drowsiness. In fact the same students that had their heads down during my presentation exited the room as though they were members of the track team.

It didn't matter though, because a larger number of students stopped to say thanks, or to say they enjoyed my presentation, or just to shake my hand. And as for the students who had their heads down, I understand that *"all closed eyes are not asleep."* I understand that if they heard the bell, they heard the presentation, and I'm certain that some of them actually *'listened.'* I understand that to actually pay attention and let other people realize that they were paying attention would have been like an assault on the perceived *'manhood'* of these young men.

These students needed to prove to others that they had everything under control. They needed to prove that they already knew what was necessary. They needed a *Power of Association* of their own, and they were not conditioned to expect it to be manifested in the African American male image that was standing in front of the class. Their imagined *Power of Association* was in the relationships with other young men and young women seeking acceptance in a society which has often prejudged and isolated them based upon age, race or other invalid criteria.

I am reminded of a good friend of mine who would attend my presentations to adult audiences with his wife Val. Eddie would always be looking around, or down, or somewhere, causing me to believe that he was disinterested or bored. But Eddie always knew more about what I had said than many who were looking right into my mouth. Eddie unfortunately passed at a rather young age, but part of my memory of him was how supportive he always was, without making an issue of that support.

Once I realized the way he paid attention was just different from what I expected, I simply modified my expectations and thanked God that Eddie was in my audience almost every time I spoke locally. He empowered me to continue. Don't allow closed eyes to detract you from what you are doing. If you believe strongly enough in something, put it out there. Some will get it then, others will get it later, and some will never get it. But regardless of the details of when and where, you will have implemented to the best of your ability *The Power of Association.*

Speaking in the Garfield Heights City School System provided a unique challenge for me. I was more accustomed to speaking to African American audiences because they are the ones who first hired me.   I was comfortable and familiar with general audiences, but Garfield Heights was different.   The school system was 14% minority and only 11% African American, and I was called upon to do a Black History Program.   Now for that, I really had to reach for another level.   I developed a presentation that I believed would demonstrate why knowledge of Black History was good for everyone.

I was cautioned by one school administrator that some white students were planning a walkout. He informed me that there were some elements whose thoughts and expressions bordered on Nazi teachings and the students had said so themselves. We both agreed that a peaceful walkout would be preferable to disruption and possible violence. The potentially disruptive element decided to stay away rather than to walk out, so all went well. A few of the white students looked bored, some I couldn't read and a few congratulated me after the program. The program went over better than I expected. The African American students were overjoyed that I could come in and share just a little of their long overlooked history. One young lady expressed her joy with an unexpected but very welcome hug. I left with the warm comfortable feeling that I had made a difference.

Believe it or not, there are schools where an offer to speak to the students is simply ignored. During the time when I had a full time job and could afford to speak for nothing, I decided that I needed to *'give back'* to the junior high school that I attended when I was a teenager. That school, Empire Jr. High was no longer a Jr. High, but I understand that it was considered a *'special focus'* elementary school, specializing in computer education.

Imagine my surprise when two letters and several phone calls to the principal went unacknowledged. One fact to keep in mind when you are trying to create positive change is that everyone is not going to understand, acknowledge or appreciate your efforts. For whatever reason, the school administration at that point and time was not *'tuned in'* to my frequency.

My message to you is that when you are faced with these unbelievable situations, remember that **The Power of Association** would have you to knock on another door, ring another telephone or do whatever is necessary for you to continue to develop and exercise that power and purpose that you believe in. Certainly my message to an audience in the surroundings which absorbed three years of my life would probably have been more relevant and powerful than the ones I've shared at John D. Rockefeller. But according to the feedback I received from the students and the parent at John D. Rockefeller, I was where I was supposed to be, speaking to those I should have been speaking to, saying what needed to be said at that time and place. **The Power of Association** was more knowing and powerful than my own understanding. That is why we are guided by the wisdom of a higher power.

Whatever your field of expertise, consider going into the school system where you live or work and spending time there. This is an area where we definitely need the advantages of **The Power of Association**. We are the children's future, and they are our future.

- SECTION EIGHT -

OTHER POWERFUL INDIVIDUALS

Supporters, Cheerleaders and Others

Congratulations

and

Thank You

Supporters, Cheerleaders and Others

Congratulations to *Anne Chapman*, supervisor at Auburn Career Center for being awarded The Ohio Administrator of the Year.

Congratulations to the co-owners of Fowler Fashions. They have made it against the odds. *Renay and Tracey Fowler* are young, female and African American. People with small minds might well call that three strikes and you're out. But Renay and Tracey are hitting home runs, and they are headed for the major leagues. These two young ladies design and make clothes, and travel nationwide in search of quality and style. It shows in the designs that they wear. I understand from people who know Renay that she is an excellent advertisement for Fowler Fashions, so I'm letting you know what I heard. I see Tracey often, and there is seldom an occasion when she doesn't look the part of a New York fashion model. So that isn't based on what I've heard, but what I've seen!

Fowler Fashions sells everything from jeans to formals. Their customers span a wide range of age and occupation. They have made clothes for entertainers such as Barry White, Men-at-Large and the ever popular Levert. Fowler Fashions is at 14476 Euclid Avenue, East Cleveland, Ohio (216) 249-8909.

Congratulations to *Sylvia Little-Harris* on your persistence in pursuing the goal of business ownership. Thanks for bringing top quality artwork to the African American community.

Congratulations to *Allison Walters* for being such a powerful role model to young African Americans. Thanks for remembering Dianne and I on special occasions.

Thank You

Arthur Abrams, Marilyn Adams, Roseanne Adams, Todd Adams, Muhammad Ahmad, Linda Alexander, Tyrone Alexander, Tynita Anderson, Renee Armstead, Hydrick & Shelley Armstrong, Eleanor Askew, Connie Atkins, Lynn Avery

Joe & Robbyn Baddour, Rick Baker Jr, Rick Sr. & Valerie Baker, Tiffany Baker, Dwayne Baldrich, Ors Banhidy, Dorothy Banks, Michelle Battle, Debbie Beckwith, Darryl & Amy Bednarski, Jim & Barbara Beidle, Dave Belle, Barry & Sandi Bennett, Fletcher Berger, Ron Berhent, James Berry, Ron Berry, Renee Bickerstaff, Sandra Bishop, Ronney Black, Virginia Black, Kenneth Blackman, Toni Blackman, John Bland, Ed Blunt Jr, Portia Blunt, Roma Blunt, Beverly Boatman, Albertine Boclear, Kim Bogan, Lillian Bogan, Richard Bolden, Martha Bonner, Robert Booker Jr., Robert Sr. & Lynda Booker, Velma Booker, Cecil Boone, Joyce Bradford, Amy Breckridge, Patricia Brim, John Brodeeck, Columbus Brown, Gladys Brown, Gloria Brown, Kenneth Brown, Larry & Carla Brown, Thomas Brown, Valia Brown, Prince Ann Brumfield, Evelyn Bryant, Marion Bryant, Aaron & Leila Bryson, Sandra Buckner, Terri Burkart, Pamela Burke, Terri Burkhart, Velma Burnett, Marlin & Wanda Burress, Keith Bush, Claude Butler, Glenn & Carolyn Byers, Loretta Byers

Joseph Caffey, Fred Caffie, Martha Caffie, Emma Caldwell, Debra Cameron, Bill & Dorothy Campbell, Joe & Zenobia Cardwell, Vernell Carey, Pam Carr, Kathryn Carter, JoAnne Carwithen, Scotland & Julia Cassell, Tommie Cave, Jeanette Chamberlin, Ronald Chambers, Robert & Anne Chapman, Vivian Chapman, John Chilkcutt, Betty Cleckley, Mack Clemmons, Arthur Coates, Charla Coleman, Calvin Cooley, Lywanna Cooper, Alice Cornett, Archie & Catherine Cotton, Glenn Cotton, Jimmy & Barbara Cozart, Vanilla Crews, Penny Croom, James Crosby, Sherry Crosby, William Crosby Jr., Thomas Crouser, Ronald & Carol Crudup, Ellen Curry, Matthew Curry

Kimberly Darks, Bill & Eloise Darling, Desi Darlington, Ethel Darlington, Alice Davis, Doris Davis, Lytle & Betty Davis, Norman Davis, Nate DeLaughter, Larry DiAngi, Reba Dickey, Harold & Joyce Dickson, Shandora Dickson, Vernest Dickson, Patrick Donadio, Marva Donerson, Carolyn Dorsey, Dr. Janice Douglas, Rita Dove, James & Karen Dozier, Pat DuBois, Gwen Dukes, Helen Dunn, Darcy Durrah

Jack & Joyce Eddington, Doris Edwards, George Edwards, Randolph Edwards, Tim & Virginia Edwards, Alice Elliott, Tina Elliott, Reginald

Ellis, Esther English, Anthony Epps, Joannie Evans, Karine Evans, Larry Evans, Jean Ezell

James & Shirley Fairley, Gary & Sheila Fannin, Jacquelyn Farley, Gloria Farris, Donna Fellow, Sylvester Ferguson, Len Ferrante, Mattie Fisher, Linda Fitzpatrick, Tim Fleming, Tico Jean Flores, Charlie & Freddie Ford, Daisy Ford, David Ford, Derek Ford, Henry Lawrence Ford, Hudson Jr. & Hilda Ford, Lawrence & Brenda Ford, Lula Mae Ford, Rebecca Ford, Robert Jr. & Laquita Ford, Willa Mae Ford, Willie Jr. & Mable Ford, Hugh Forde, Horrace Foster, Reginald Foster, Toni Francis, Sarah Franklin, Charlie Freeman, Craig Freeman

Mittie Gamble, Abdul Ghani, Margaret Gibson, Michael & Maryanne Gill, Bethany Gilmore, Claudia Gindraw, Joanne Gleghorn, John & Beverly Glover, Jody Goggans, Randy & Angela Goode, Corrine Goodwin, Ruby Grant, Judy Guthrie

John Hada, Charlie Hall, Dee Hall, Wade & Frankie Hamilton, Chris Hampton, Lenora Hancock, Daryl Hanson, Tom & Eloise Hardin, Leonard Hardy, Yulanda Hardy, Marcia Harris, Orvita Harris, Patricia Harris, Hallie Hart, Kelly Hart, Teri Hatton, Diana Havel, Ronald & Dora Jean Havrilla, Michelle Hawkins, Chuck & Jenny Heldreth, DoLores Henderson, Sam & Leontyne Henderson, Eloise Henry, Mike & Charlene Herchick, John & Fannie Herritage, Noah Hester, Valerie Hicks, Wayne Hicks, Walter Hodge, Mark & Susan Hofener, Ann Holman, Doug Jr. & Evelyn Holmes, Doug Sr. & LaVerne Holmes, Vernon & Cathy Holmes, Alton Holsey, Deontaye Holsey, Melba Holsey, Tanya Holsey, Mary Holt, Richard Holt, Tim Houston, Myra Howell, Z. Ann Hoyle, Andrea Hudson, Andrick Hudson, Dorothy Hudson, Kevin Hudson, Mary Hudson, Rhea Hudson, Linda Hunter, Regina Hutchings, Cheryl Hutchins

Joyce Ingram, Emanuel & Sylvia Irby, Howard & Judy Ivary

James & Tayaba Jackson, Kevin Jackson & Arlene Jackson, Rasool Jackson & JoAnn Ford, Renee Jackson, Tony & Gwen Jackson, Delphine James, Ralph & Susan Jarosz, Leon & Betty Jenkins, Charles & J.B. Jernigan, Aaron & Debra Johnson, Charles & Myra Johnson, Eloise Johnson, Gerald Johnson, Janice Johnson, Lisa Johnson, Olivia Johnson, Richard & Rosetta Johnson, Robert Johnson, Tiny Johnson, Celia Jones, Dorothy Jones, James & Sherbia Jones, Janice Jones, June Jones, Ken Jones, Kevin Jones, Mary Jones, Carmen Josey, Jim Joyner

Ernest Kelly, Dr. Velta Kelly, Crystal Kelso, George Kendall, George Kenyon, Terri Kenzig, Barry Kerrigan, William & Mattie Kidd, Carolyn Kimble, William King, Kurt Klingman, Kevin Knuckles, Mary Kohns, Kip & Linda Kuebler, Richard & Linda Kulaga

Nancy Lahodny, Cindy Lamar, Jeanette Langford, Vivian Laster, Spencer Lattimore, Hank Lawson, Rose Lawson, Sherman & Benora Lee, Dody Lesco, Creasie Lewis, Eunice Lewis, Marcia Lewis, Minnie Lewis, Josie Lindsay, Kathleen Lindsay, Connie Little, Nardalisa Little, Alfred & Margaret Littman, Cheryl Long, Earl Lumpkin, Jay & Jane Luteran, Rev. Webster Lytle

Rev. Larry Macon, Denise Mahone, Robert Manley, Eugene & Theckla Mann, Rosella Marilao, Dorothy Martin, Marby Matheus, Johnnie McAnulty, Betty McCall, Gerry McClamy, Mel McCray, Jackie McDonald, Janis McGregor, Barbara Middleton, David Middleton, Ernest & Lillie Miller, Gloria Miller, Ronnie Miller, Ernestine Mills, Larry Minter, Charles & Ruth Mitchell, Deirdre Mitchell, Lita Mitchell, James & Marcia Mockabee, Michelle Mockabee, Jamal & Alice Mohammed, Mary Molton, Margaret Monroe, Charles & Lynn Montgomery, Gigi Moore, Betty Morgan, Evie Morganfield, Gloria Morganfield, Leo Moskovsky, Michael & Janet Mullens, James Myers, Chris Myrick, Gwennie Myricks

Barbara Nabors, Sandra Noble, Lloyd & Barbara Noles, Dorothy Norwood, Debra Nunn, Judy Nye

Ray Odom, William & Gloria O'Neal, Jennifer Opperman, Debbie Owens, Yolanda Owens

Lavonia Paige, Jill Parham, Ida Paul, Euneta Payne, Barbara Peck, Sue Pellini, Jodi Pengal, Tanya Penn, Willie Peterson, Sheila Petty, Gail Phillips, Howard Pincham, Celesta Pless, Pamela Poindexter, Tangy Poindexter, Louis Prekop, Leon Pryor

Ken Raines, Val Randle, Richard Raypole, Kristen Reed, Danette Render, Norman & Helen Reynolds, Bobbylyne Rice, Sonny & Carol Richards, Gerri Richardson, Karen Richardson, Ed & Karen Rimmer, Mary Roberts, Connie Roland, Mark Robinson, Dorothy Rodgers, Dorothy Rogers, Renaldo Rogers, Stephen Rowan, Tom Rudar

Dr. Mohammad Saleem, Olivia Sauvey, Janet Schmitz, Marilyn Schott, Ameenah Shafeeq, Hassana Shareef, Shirley Sharp, Michael & Marian Shaughnessy, Linda Shelton, Marilyn Schott, David Shipley, Pete Shomade,

Barbara Simmons-Holmes, Zel Sinclair, Emma Slayton, Tim Smart, Alice Smith, Allison Smith, Doris Smith, Dorothy Smith, Greg Smith, James & Eleanor Smith, Jason Smith, Mary Smith, Paula Smith, Stacie Smith, Robert & Joan Snead, Kirby and Myra Snipes, Teresa Snoddy, Demo Solaru, Paula Stanley, JoAnne Stevens, Burma Stewart, Floyd & Betty Stewart, Henry & Carrie Stewart, Thomas & Mildred Stith, John Story, Lennie Stover, Mike & Cindy Strang, Marion Styles, Cassandra Suttles, Patty Sykes

Sharon Tanner, Dennis & Laura Tavenier, Ethel Taylor, Joe & June Taylor, Juanita Taylor, Patty Taylor, William & Marilyn Taylor, Shirletha Taylor-Green, Gary & Carol Thobaben, Eric Thomas, Gerald & Sharon Thomas, Grover Thomas Sr., Henry & Laura Thomas, Jerry & Valerie Thomas, Louise Thomas, Michael Thomas, Nicole Thomas, Pat Thomas, Henry & Ellen Thompson, Janet Thompson, Zachary & Carolyn Thompson, Alvin Thorton, Tom Threat, Patricia Thurmond, Barbara Trevis, John Trevis, Hazel Troupe, Dave & Mary Jo Truman, Portia Tuck, Chester Tucker, Joyce Tucker, Joyce Tuggle, Cornelius Turner, Mary Turner, James & Evangeline Tyler

Melanie Valentine, Maria Valle, Suzanne Vaughan, Peggy Vauss, Charlotte Vennekohl, Dorothy Vianos, Mattie Vinson, Willie & Margaret Vinson, Willie & Sarah Vinson, Pat Vujtech

Joyce Wagoner, Rogena Walden, James & Charlotte Walter, Terrance Walton, Ron & Marilyn Ward, Deborah Warner, Wil & Tabitha Warren, Ed & Susan Washington, Jo Ann Weaver, Thelma Wells, Richard & Freda West, Gordon & Cindy Weston, Keeouko Whaley, Josie White, Willie White, Barbara Whitfield, Sharilyn Whitley, Ardell Whitworth, Sharron Wiggins, Ike & Sheila Wilkerson, Robert & Deirdre Wilkes, Richard Wilkins, Leon Wilkinson, Angie Williams, Anthony Williams, Charles Williams, George Williams, Harvey & Pearl Williams, Judy Williams, Leonard & Etta Williams, Lillian Williams, Sheila Williams, Al & Mary Williamson, Johnnie Williamson, Janis Willis, Sally Willis, Bernice Wilson, Eric Wilson, Katie Wilson, Kenneth & Debra Wilson, Tom Wilson, Phillip & Casandra Wingfield, Gary Wise, Dee Wooden

Bob & Christine Young, Ed Young, Tan Young

Richard & Dianne Zalack, Michael & Dorothy Zivick

Sorry Folks, we just ran out of room! If we missed you and we shouldn't have, please print your name below and we will sign next to it.

- SECTION NINE -
Contributing Writers

Cassie Adams-Lewis

Harvey Alston

SeMia Bray

Angela Craft

Maurice Curlee

Dianne Ford

Robert L. Lawson

Lucius Lewis

Aleta Mays

Ilinda Reese

Patricia Wingard Carson

"Variety has been described as 'the spice of life.'
So sit back, open your minds, and allow the spice
to flavor your intellect and your imagination."

"That taught me the lesson of how important it is to know from where you came and who you are. "

- Cassie L. Adams-Lewis -

Letter To A Real Role Model
August, 1995

This piece is dedicated to a generation that chooses television personalities, sports figures, or those who make fast money as role models. Take a look in your own backyard to find good role models.

> You made it possible for me to tell a junior high school counselor that I was going to college anyway after she told me that I should be a *"bookkeeper or something,"* because she *thought* my grades weren't good enough. That was in 1965. I was fourteen years old.

> I remember you telling me why and how your family migrated north. My grandparents were sharecroppers in Georgia and like most, could not provide for their family. One day, my grandfather drove his horse and wagon into town to conduct *"business."* That business turned out to be a train ride destined for Ohio's steel mills. Since you were just a baby, you didn't know how long it was before you, your eight sisters and brothers, and mother, came to join him. When my grandfather finally sent for his family, my grandmother, a big woman managed to hide some of her nine children under her skirts in order to board that train. She didn't have fare for everyone. That taught me a lesson in determination.

> You were just four years old when your mother died. When family members told my grandfather that they

were willing to help him by taking *some* of his children, he replied with, *"If I can keep one, I can keep all ten."* He later took in two young nephews when their parents chose to abandon them. That taught me a lesson in giving and sharing.

You were barely 16 and in the ninth grade when you were forced to drop out of school, because my grandfather had died. You began taking care of yourself. I remember the stories you told me of your first jobs. One in particular that stands out in my mind is when you cleaned homes for white people. You told me that one day a woman for whom you worked, told you, not asked, but told you to tie her mother's shoes. As you knelt, the old woman asked, *"Where's your mammy?"* You replied (no doubt, in your standard English voice) with, *"If you're talking about my mother, she died when I was four, I've never had a mammy."* That taught me the lesson of how important it is to know from where you came and *who* you are.

You told me how you would work all night and went to beauty school during the day. You would be so tired, that you could stand up and sleep while on the bus. That didn't seem to matter, because you soon earned your cosmetology and manager's license. That taught me a lesson that if it was easy, everyone would do it.

Jackie was barely three, Russell fifteen months, and Marcel six-weeks old, and I hadn't even been born when you started your own business at home. That was in 1949. My father objected, but you convinced him that it was the right thing to do. He became accustomed to the clicking of the curling irons and the curious smells after coming home from the steel mills. You told me that oftentimes, before leaving for work, he would have washed clothes and hung them out to dry before you woke up in the morning. If the greens were simmering, he cooked the hot-water cornbread. If you bathed the first two, he bathed the last two. You proved that balancing career and family was evident even then. You taught me the lesson that a family is as strong as they choose to be.

I was six when my father died in a car accident. That was in 1959. You were only 38 years old. Four years later, President Kennedy was assassinated. I often compared you to Jackie Kennedy. You were a single parent long before single mothers were viewed to be able to raise only gang members and pregnant teens. You stepped in and were both mother and father to us. The lesson I learned was that parenting and family life are to be taken seriously.

When you decided to move your business out of your house, you didn't take balance sheets or a business plan to the bank for a loan. Not for one moment did you think you couldn't do it. Rather, you prayed and asked God to lead you in the right direction.

Thanks Mom

Author's Comment - Now you see why I like her! Cassie is quiet for a speaker and trainer, but knowledgeable, insightful, with a demonstrated ability to deliver the message. She is always, always, always ready to strengthen weak hearts and challenge narrow minds. Cassie could easily be called, and has been called the conscience of *Worth Sharing Communications*. She is the Executive Director of Women Working for Self-Employment of Cleveland. For more information you may contact Cassie at 216-663-4866 or write to her at 5311 Northfield Rd #221, Bedford Hts, OH 44146.

- Harvey Alston -

"A Close Association Brings About Assimilation"

There are many fine quotes on the power of association and most of them are true. When one becomes close to a person they begin to take on some of their attributes, mannerisms, gestures, and even the very words or phrases are the same. Young couples who spend countless hours together soon find that they start to look like each other. Actually they begin to talk, walk, and act in a similar manner which outsiders conclude that they look alike. Couples who have been married for many years find that one partner can start a sentence and the other mate can finish it without a pause. They have been around each other so long that their very thinking patterns are the same. They eat the same food, look at the same programs, go to bed at the same time, and wake up each day with each other. A close association truly brings about an assimilation.

"Birds of a Feather Flock Together"

If you are looking for success in your own life find a group of successful people to hang around or become part of their group or circle. In many different clubs or organizations you will find a large group who share a common vision or goal. In some clubs or organizations their purpose or creed is based on community needs where you will find a very homogeneous group. The average age of the group will not differ in extremes. The average income and life styles will not vary much on the scale. People who have somewhat the same style of worship will attend the same type of church. Birds of a feather will flock together.

"Water Seeks Its Own Level"

Whatever you have chosen in life as your vocation, career, or life's work, you will find yourself with friends and associates whose work and economic rewards are close to yours. The very minute that one person in this circle grows to a higher level in their profession and income, they no longer fit in that group. If they were your drinking friends at the bar, they move up to the country club. When you cook-out, they eat out. When you load the kids in the wagon for the trip to the Zoo, they fly to Las Vegas for the weekend. It is at this point that both of you know you have grown apart and it's time to seek friends on you own level.

"If You Hang Around With Trash, You'll Begin To Stink"

Just as good friendships and associations can lift you to a higher ground, bad relationships with friends or loved ones can knock you off the road to success and drag you downhill to crawl in the mud at the bottom. Every parent who's loving child, they find in deep trouble, the first word out of their mouth is *"I knew he was going to get in trouble because he was hanging around with the wrong group of people."* This proud mother has rejected the fact that once a child associates with this group he becomes part of that same group. He is not hanging out with bad kids, he has become a bad kid. If you go out with people who do drugs, people will think you do drugs. If you hang out with people who steal then people will think you are a thief. If you listen to ethnic jokes, people will think you are racist.

"You Are Known By The Company You Keep"

If we are to be judged in this life, not only by our deeds, but by the deeds of others, then it makes all the sense in the world for us to empower our future by carefully selecting those that we associate with. As I was trying to start my own business I found many friends and associates to help me along the way. One of these outstanding groups was the Boy Scouts of America. As a member of the Advisory Board I met many new friends whose love for helping young men were in line with my goals for raising my two sons.

I found that while serving as Vice President of a Kiwanis Club I learned how to run meetings more effectively, and how to motivate people to work for a common good. Being a member of the Chamber of Commerce put me in touch with business people of all walks of life. I sat at the conference table with presidents of Fortune 500 Companies while at the same time with the sole owner of a mom and pop store. The Adopt-A-School Program, Keep Ohio Beautiful Commission, Advisory Board, Southeast Career Center, Board Member, Friends of the Library, Career Education Association, Ohio Speaker's Forum, and the National Speakers Association have all lifted me and I have received much more than I have given.

Surround yourself with the best people that can assist you in becoming your BEST.

HARVEY ALSTON, PRESIDENT
BEST, INC. - 2665 Mitzi Drive - Columbus, OH 43209
(614) 235-5411

Author's Comments - Trying to define or describe Harvey Alston is like a man who nearly drowned telling you how much he appreciated the lifeboat. On the voyage of success, whether you are facing the obvious challenges of rough seas, or the hidden dangers of tranquil waters, you will need access to a unique combination of wit, wisdom, competence and willingness to help. Harvey Alston is that unique and priceless combination, and more! He is not only the Captain of his ship, but also the first mate of countless others. Thanks Harvey.

"Many times we are held prisoner by our own negative perceptions of what is happening around us. When in actuality we have the opportunity to step through 'the door' and become empowered to accomplish worthwhile goals. As we dream, so be it."

- SeMia Bray -

Success in Diversity: You Can Be #1, too. . .

Some may be asking, how is it that *"You Can Be #1, too..."*? The answer lies within the notion that each of us has a unique contribution that no one else can fulfill.   It is from this perspective that we focus on individual success. Each one of us was created unique.   No two people, not even identical twins can stand face to face and proclaim they are the same. It is this very uniqueness that gives life its spice and is the essence of diversity that links us all together. As each of us travel upon our personal journey of success, I am mindful that we all have something to contribute that will make our lives significant. As we strive to be the best we can be, we move closer to being #1. No one else can out perform us as #1 at being ourselves. And the wonderful thing is, there is enough individuality available that we all can think of ways to be #1 according to our own standard.

With this in mind, there are those who are stronger at some skills than others. However, when you look at all that we have to contribute, each one of us has something of value to offer. We all have a success story waiting to unfold. The dilemma is many people do not exercise this freedom due to continuous negative programming.

Negative programming is that voice inside us all rooted in self doubt and insecurity. It is this programming that reminds us of what we can not do or achieve.   True, we can not control everything that occurs in our lives but we can control how we process what happens and how we choose to respond. I believe Hugh Downs said it best when he stated, *"A happy person is not a person in a certain set of circumstances, but rather a person with a certain set of attitudes."*

We get better at what we practice most. If we focus on the negative occurrences in life, then we will become experts at finding what is wrong with everything. Conversely, if we focus on the positive, we find that life continually brings us opportunities. I would not insult you and suggest that we have to be happy all the time. However, research shows that those who exercise responsibility for their own responses tend to bounce back more completely from adversity and learn more from the experience.

I am reminded of a story where a prisoner was being prepared for execution. On the day he was to die, he was given the choice to be executed or go through a door labeled *"Unknown horrors."* He chose execution. Afterwards the question was asked, *"What was behind the door?"*   The answer, *"FREEDOM."*

The prison represents the emotional restraints we put upon ourselves through self doubt and insecurity. Each and every one of us has experienced negative programming through our own lenses of experience. Many times we are held prisoner by our own negative perceptions of what is happening around us. When in actuality we have the opportunity to step through *"the door"* and become empowered to accomplish worthwhile goals. As we dream, so be it.

Stretch out and take a chance.   You can not discover new oceans if you do not have courage to lose sight of the shore. So while you are doing your inner work, remember the more you learn about yourself the more willing you become to learn about others. And the more you learn about others, the more you realize about yourself. By understanding the uniqueness in the experiences of others, we add one more tool to our *"tool box"* of skills on the road to success. Make a commitment to yourself to be one of those people who stand up and make things happen. Be a person that can look back over their life and say, *"I have truly made my mark and lived my dreams to the fullest."* Success is a journey, not a destination. Enjoy the trip...

Author's Comment - SeMia is an intuitive, dynamic speaker and individual who truly sets the standard of excellence. A business consultant, lecturer and community servant, her message is penetrating and powerful.   After listening to her speak, I decided that she should carry a warning label that states, *"Audience must retain fire extinguishers and fasten seat belts before listening."*

For more information you may contact SeMia at

> Cray Consulting Group
> P.O. Box 28498
> Cleveland, OH 44128
> (216) 556-1745

"Through positive association, a very powerful web of support is created so that failure is not an option."

- Angela Craft -

Succeeding By The Numbers

Through the power of association, every individual is given the opportunity to challenge the dreams of tomorrow with their realisms of today. Negativity is all around us, and in no short supply. We see examples of it daily on the television, and hear it constantly in our everyday dealings with others. Rather than give into the negative energy; refusing to silently acquiesce to the depths of despair, and realizing that lack of growth leads to stagnation, it is only by natural instinct we surround ourselves with others. Those individuals tend to be most like ourselves, with positive aspirations and lofty visions.

Sharing the uniqueness that each one of us has to offer through association with others helps every individual benefit, and increases their personal growth. Continually growing through personal development enables us to succeed where others might have never dared to go, accomplishing tasks that many might have deemed impossible, and to ultimately and triumphantly beat the odds. Having the stamina to consistently pursue a dream despite what some would say are overwhelming odds, takes a lot of inner strength. Trying to self motivate during times of turmoil or continual rejection is a lot easier when one or more individuals are there as a supportive group. Through positive association, a very powerful web of support is created so that failure is not an option.

This network acts as an outlet for creative ideas and plausible solutions, and it also acts as an inlet with the sharing of ideas and visions. This type of association can therefore be compared to a two-way street. Just as traffic flows in both directions, in a supportive network ideas and praise can also flow freely. Often times, as on a two-way street, people must realize that the road may be full of bumps and potholes, and extreme caution is needed to navigate through successfully.

Sometimes when you set out on a journey and you're not quite sure of where it is you are going, if you're going to make it there safely and honestly, if you even really want to go, it's a little hard to get started. Unfortunately the drawback to riding solo is that it leaves no one to help calm the fears and give reassuring council. Without another reassuring voice, negative thoughts eat away any type of rational thought. Having a voice of reason gives light to the darkness and turns every negative into an opportunity. Having someone to travel the journey with, willing to share in the experience makes everything a lot less frightening. Realizing someone is there for you helps to lessen the burden, and provide a foundation for success.

It is therefore my strong belief based on personal experiences as well as testimonials from old friends, that the old saying of safety in numbers holds true. Having a select group of individuals all focused on a common goal, all believing in the same vision is a powerful force not to be reckoned with. Someone once said a few with belief is far more greater than a force of ninety-nine with mere interests. Therefore, positive association can benefit an individual as well as uplift an entire group and lead them that much closer to the success they seek.

Author's Comment - Angela Craft is the invisible part of that younger generation that we seldom hear about or read about. The part that is educated, competent and solution focused. She brings to her audiences a refreshing breath of relief and a strong dose of belief.   Angela brings this antibiotic at a time when many are suffering the plagues of hopelessness and stagnation.

Angela may be contacted at

Cray Consulting Group
P.O. Box 28498
Cleveland, OH 44128
(216) 556-1745

"I believe that it is imperative to have powerful thoughts, simply because a thought is the beginning of all reality."

- Maurice C. Curlee -

On Associations

I can recall vividly crying out to my ex-wife one summer day after jogging perhaps five miles and feeling exceptionally good about myself. My endorphins had just given me the pleasure of the runner's *'high.'* I can't quite recall the topic of the conversation that gave me the courage to dig deep down inside of my emotional bank vault and to actually verbalize that *"I am worthy"* of more than I was getting from that relationship and for that matter more than I was getting out of life. I truly do not believe that my wife at the time realized the significance of those three little words; *"I am worthy."* For me it was the moment that I began to embrace the fact that I had potential and a sense of self that suggested that I deserved more than I was experiencing in my life. From that day forth I have not only embraced this knowingness, but I have committed myself to doing whatever is necessary for me to achieve whatever goal that I am worthy of seeding and achieving.

I believe that it is imperative to have powerful thoughts, simply because a thought is the beginning of all reality. You see. . .I once had a powerful thought that I was going to wake up one morning and my mother would leave my life without a trace and I would be all alone. This thought was given to me by my mother. Let me explain. My mother often suffered from depression and most of the depression stemmed from the association she had with my father. I believe strongly that my father did not want children, but because he had children he begrudingly took on the responsibility of raising a family. Often my father would drink and associate with people beneath his potential and station in life. These associations took him out of the home and into the streets and ultimately away from my mother. So in times of utter despair my mother would lament that someday she would simply walk away. I'm sure you can visualize the emotional impact this had on my young mind.

In an effort to keep my mother from leaving me, I became the good little boy, the achiever and the depressed little boy who would come home after school and watch the *Days of Our Lives, As The World Turns* and *General Hospital* with my depressed mother. You could say that my association with my mother was based on anger and just being stuck.

I have learned in the past eleven years of my recovery from alcohol and drugs that my associations will have an immense effect on my life experience. I also believe that we are who we are because of the people that love us and those who choose not to love us. It is very simple, it is impossible to live on this planet without another person. God did not make us that way. *"Man cannot live by bread alone"* says one of the scriptures.

As I reflect back on my relationship with my ex-wife, I now know that she was a blessing for me. She in fact helped me to feel a personal worth, with a belief that I was truly worthy and ultimately helped to do worthwhile deeds while helping me to form healthy associations with worthwhile people such as; Cassie Adams-Lewis, Peter Bell, Alexandria Boone, SeMia Bray, Les Brown, Berry Gordy, Henry Ford, George Fraser, Dr. Maulana Karenga, Jawanza Kunjufu, Lucius Lewis, Felix H. Liddell, Ilinda Reese and many others. I have no doubt that I will continue to experience healthy relationships on a daily basis simple because I know now that I am a worthy human being, capable of extraordinary deeds.

One of my Ten Steps of success and happiness is: To expect the best from every encounter. I know that every encounter with another human being is a blessing and holy. How can that be when we have strife and hatred among mankind? Simply put, if there is hatred, there is always an opportunity to change the condition with love. I have found that if a person is angry for some reason that he or she feels justified for being in that particular state. To react in a loving way to that hate with loving energy somehow dismantales that hateful energy within that individual. In times of stress, what comes out of us is actually what is inside of us. Human beings have the unique capacity to change. Therefore if we find that there is anger, we can change that energy into another form of energy if we choose, such as a loving positive energy. The most phenomenal aspect of energy is that it is only energy as long as it is in the company of ourselves and another human being or an association.

Associations makes reality. I could not have achieved the success in my life that I now experience if it had not been for my desire to come out of the abyss of my emotional pain. Healthy associations as well as toxic associations are keeping me on my journey to personal worthiness. Speaking of toxic associations, they too are blessings. For me toxic associations let me know what I don't want for my reality. They remind me that if I maintain a toxic association, I will invariably return to a toxic lifestyle such as drinking and drugging. The question then arises, am I worthy of success and happiness? And am I worthwhile in achieving more, doing more and having more? At this moment in time we are only worth what we are receiving at this moment in time. We will receive more when we feel worthy of receiving and experiencing more.

In my upcoming book _You Are Truly Worthy!_ I will share my personal history of childhood pain, a life of addiction and recovery, personal achievements and the steps that I developed to accomplish some of my life goals.

Isn't life wonderful? And if you think it can be better, you're right! All you have to do is believe that you are worthy simply because you showed up on this planet.

I want to thank Henry Ford for the opportunity to share with you some of my thoughts on this wonderful subject of **Associations** and my brief introduction to my upcoming book *You are Truly Worthy*. It is important to realize that there can be nothing that exists without another person. I challenge you to develop and nurture healthy relationships, but most importantly with yourself. Create the all-knowingness within you. **That You Are A Worthy Person and allow the magic to happen!**

Thank you again Henry for our association and the opportunity to contribute to your wonderful book.

Author's Comment - Maurice Curlee, M.Ed has obviously journeyed from the depths of despair to the heights of enlightened accomplishment. He understands as we all must learn to, that the quality of life is fragile. He understands that even though each of us is responsible for ourselves, we are nevertheless extremely vulnerable to relationships and need to make them positive whenever possible. Maurice is a motivational speaker, educator and counseling therapist and currently the Director of Mt. Sinai/Laurelwood's Mental Health & Chemical Dependency Treatment Program.

You can contact Maurice at

> 13719 S. Parkway Drive
> Garfield Hts., OH 44105
> (216) 581-9559

"If we expect to receive the power of association, we must also be willing to give it. That is the way God planned it, that is why we are not here alone."

- Dianne Ford -

New And Old Friends

For the purposes of this story, I am expanding the term friends to include relatives, business associates and casual acquaintances.

Whether our relationship is personal or business, casual or serious, frequent or seldom, our *friends* can affect how we think, how we feel, how we act. They can affect how happy we are, or if we are happy at all. They can affect how fast we grow, or if we grow at all.

In life, you will find many types of *friends*. Some will cause you to stumble and fall, and often they won't care at all. Others will help you to stand tall, they are usually as close as a call. Since you have the choice, it makes sense to choose as wisely as possible and then do all you can to make that choice work.

We are aware of the figure of speech *"Make new friends and keep the old, one is silver and the other gold."* An important lesson in the power of association is that both silver and gold are precious metals.

We need to treat our friendships like precious metal, and understand that they are to be chosen carefully, cherished and protected from harm. They should not be thrown around or given harsh treatment. They should not be pushed and stretched beyond their limits. They should not be forsaken in favor of something with more glitter.

Life is a continuous journey. On that journey are roadblocks, detours, bad weather and other hazards. Sometimes there are the unexpected results of bad relationships. Warning us of those hazards are caution signs, roadmaps, information booths and occasionally an arresting officer or a presiding judge.

Our choice of personal relationships determines how well our trip might go. If we break down on the highway, have we developed the kind of relationships that will stop and give us a tow? Or will they call 911 for assistance? Or will they simply drive on by?

What about us, what if we spot our friend on the berm, temporarily out of gas or in need of a mental tuneup. In our hurry to get to the next destination, will we offer assistance, or get into the fast lane and expect someone else to stop and help?

If God is our co-pilot, and we have developed the right spiritual association, chances are that we will stop and help that friend. If we fail in that association, we should understand that just ahead on the road might be the loneliness of a darkened highway, with all those who passed us by somewhere ahead, and all those we passed by somewhere behind.

If we expect to receive the power of association, we must also be willing to give it. That is the way God planned it, that is why we are not here alone.

Learning and listening to others, expressing and absorbing feelings, sharing the pain and sorrow of others, all that helps to create your identity. What is your identity? Are you a positive association to your *friends*, or a negative one? Do your *friends* know you as a help or a hindrance? When you walk into a crowd of your *friends*, do they smile and gather closer, or do they frown and look at their watches?

The power of association is like no other power. It is not taxed and it is not affected by the *'energy crisis.'* You can't escape from it though. You can choose either the power of positve association, or the pain of negative association, the choice is yours.

Author's Comment - Anybody with any *'smarts'* knows that a husband doesn't make comments about his wife. You be the judge. I am certain she will be happy with your verdict.

"No one can consistently play in the major leagues with a minor league mentality"

- Dr. Robert L. Lawson -

Commenting on The Power of Association

Though influences are many, there are probably none that have a greater impact upon your life than do those individuals with whom you spend time. The author of this book, Henry Ford, has had the fortuitious insight to discuss a profound topic that has life changing implications. The one common denominator of all successful people lies in the fact that when their lives change for the better, it is usually as a result of changes that have taken place in their peer group.

Ralph Walso Emerson understood this concept well. This is why he and Henry David Thoreau, two great writers, had such a remarkable influence upon each other and ultimately the world. Dr. Martin Luther King Jr. understood the concept well which is why many of his nonviolent tactics are said to have been influenced by Mahatma Ghandi. Just the other night, I sat engrossed on the edge of my sofa as I watched two modern day superstarts, Jay Leno and Oprah Windrey share common experiences on the Jay Leno Show.

Successful people are drawn to each other. The more I write and speak, for example, the greater I find the results to be. Whatever the interests, desires and dreams are, the more you will have the opportunities to interact with those individuals who are of like thought and have similar aspirations.

As Les Brown, one of the world's most effective motivational speakers and I talked the other night in Columbus, Ohio, Les made a very important point. *"Bob,"* he said *"One of the most important keys to success lies in distribution. Until folks get to the point where they can understand that it's not what you know but who you know, they're not going to be as successful as they'd like to be."* Les is right. The real power of association lies in numbers.

Individuals who have a product, service, skill or talent to sell must insure that it is a quality product and make others who are in key positions aware that it is available. Harvey Alston, a good friend and mentor recently called me on the phone and asked if I could participate with him on an all day speaking program. I was not available to participate on the day he had in mind, but we plan to pursue that idea in the future.

When someone believes in you enough to share their audience with you, it's an opportunity of a lifetime. Why? Because the element of trust had been established. Business is all about building mutual trust relationships. As these relationships are built, your power base increases. You then have the opportunity to make or unmake yourself by virtue of your performance and your follow through. Those who are not genuine and do not have the qualities it takes to succeed on a major level need not worry at all because their place in the big arena will be for a limited time only. No one can consistently play in the major leagues with a minor league mentality.

Each of us has the power of choice. Those with whom we choose to associate determine whether or not we can successfully broaden our network base and our opportunities for positive business opportunities. One positive event can lead to a number of others. You must, however, be seen and heard by the right people. Increased exposure leads to even more exposure and then it will be the quality of your product or service that determines your future success. It is imperative that you keep polishing and refining your product or service in order to maintain a competitive advantage.

My speaking and writing career began to blossom as I became affiliated with the Ohio Speakers Forum and the National Speakers Association. The people involved in these organizations were people of like mind. They were interested in moving up in life, doing better and maximizing their brain power.

Soon, I was able to connect with individuals of like thought not just in Ohio, Kentucky and West Virginia, where I live and in the surrounding areas, but through both formal and informal networks. I began to receive calls from New York, Louisiana, Oklahoma, Iowas, Michigan, Washington, DC and a number of other states. In fact, through my editor, Matt Krise at the Kendall/Hunt Publishing Company in Dubuque, Iowa I have secured a number of speaking engagements, radio talk shows, book signings and T.V. shows all generated in response to two of my published books, ***Destined For Greatness*** and ***Oh, Yes We Can!*** *Black Achievement In America.*

Once the contact has been made however, I cannot stress enough how important it becomes for you to follow through. I would guess that the majority of contracts in any business endeavor are aborted for lack of follow through. In fact 50% of book contracts signed never make it into print because the potential author fails to deliver a final product. It is my hope that you, the reader, can see the importance of networking with others. Take the time to help them boost their careers as well as yours out of mutual respect and admiration and that you understand fully the power of positive association and its impacet upon the human mind.

Always remember the immortal words of Zig Ziglar. *"You can get anything you want in life if you will just help enough other people get what they want."*

And even then, if absolutely nothing turns out the way you had hoped it would, you will always be able to find comfort and solace in some of the greatest words ever written by Gandhi when he says,

> *"It's the action, not the fruit of the action that's important. You have to do the right thing. It may not be in your power, may not be in your time, that there'll be any fruit. But that doesn't mean you stop doing the right thing. You may never know what results come from your action. But if you do nothing, there will be no result."*

Author's Comment - Dr. Robert L. Lawson, a contributing author to *The Power of Association* is a member of the National Speakers Association, the Ohio Speakers Forum and has presented at many national conferences. He has authored two books through Kendall/Hunt Publishing Company, *Destined For Greatness and Oh, Yes We Can! Black Achievement in America*. The books can be ordered by calling 1-800-228-2810. Dr. Lawson can be contacted at 1809 Hall Avenue, Huntington, WV 25701 - 1-304-523-5392. His third book is currently being worked on and is due off the press in 1996. It is entitled *The Triumph of The Spirit*.

"The imagination and creative capacity of our life is sparked from the bombardment of new ideas, different strategies and the incredible potential of becoming the person you can be is exciting. New areas of personal development are explored and enhanced. "

- Lucius Lewis -

Challenge, Influence and Growth
August, 1995

The challenge of developing and maintaining balance in all areas of life is a continuous struggle. The pressures of family responsibility, financial concerns, health issues, employment instability and the incredible phenomenon of constant change keeps the average person in a state of uncertainty.

The powerful influence of good positive association provides a boost of energy and emotional support. Our fears and insecurities can be expressed in a supportive, nurturing environment. Our feelings, perceptions and perspective are validated. Conversely, when correction, readjustment and/or discipline is needed, the courage and willingness to provide such is available.

Perhaps the most beneficial aspect of good association is the connection you feel with others. Our talents and abilities have the nurturing environment conducive to accelerated personal growth.

The imagination and creative capacity of our life is sparked from the bombardment of new ideas, different strategies and the incredible potential of becoming the person you can be is exciting. New areas of personal development are explored and enhanced.

To those of you who are experiencing the benefit of good association, may you continue to do it more fully. For those of you who have thought about or are open to this tremendous opportunity for self exploration and emotional grounding, may you start your journey now!

Author's Comment - Lucius, founder of **Worth Sharing Communications**, businessman and trainer, is also the author of **_A Better Way of Taking Care of You_**. Noted international speaker Les Brown provided the foreword for that powerful personal self-development course.

For more information you may contact Lucius at (216) 752-9400 or write him in care of A.J. Lewis & Associates, 3725 Lee Road, Cleveland, OH 44120.

"I am living proof that
ONE MONKEY DON'T STOP NO SHOW!"

- Aleta Mays -

Welfare Warfare - Featuring **The Monkey** *(Welfare System),* **The Ammo** *(Divorce, education and employment)* and **The Show** *(Financial independence and control)*

When I divorced, I lost three-quarters of my income when my former husband left. I was one of the millions of women unable to collect child support, because of interstate differences in law, legal fiascos, and the inability to track and trace *"lost"* fathers. That MONKEY should have beaten me down. Instead, I found the inner strength to keep on pushing. I didn't let that MONKEY stop my SHOW. I had a dream. I had a SHOW and I had to get on with it.

I moved from California back to Ohio with a kitty, a kid, a car seat, and nine boxes. I had to make some decisions about my future and I had to make them in a hurry.

The little savings I had was exhausted by the move back east and re-establishing our new home. Much to the embarrassment of my parents who were living examples of the American work ethic, I applied for welfare.

Do you know how degrading it is to be on welfare? You lose a part of yourself to the system. You lose your privacy. You lose your individuality. You're collectively labeled *"the problem."* How do you regain self-esteem after being told you're the reason the economy is in such sad shape? How do you respond to remarks such as, *"If you'd stop having babies and get a job, then everything would be alright."* Or, *"Why don't you earn your keep and stop asking for a handout?"* Do you know how it feels to be in a grocery store check-out line and have people behind you make comments to the effect that you're lazy and good for nothing? How can you feel good about who you are? I want to let you in on a reality check. Everyone on welfare isn't a lazy bum. Every woman on welfare doesn't have baby after baby. Oh, that's what the media would like you to think, but those are the exceptions, not the rule. In fact, many folks on welfare have simply experienced a downturn in luck. Many of these recipients had jobs, but perhaps their company merged, downsized, or moved south of the border. I tell those who condemn welfare recipients, *"Don't talk about welfare unless you've been there. Don't talk about who you think these people are because many of life's circumstances could put you in a welfare line in a heartbeat."* Many Americans are one, or possibly only two paychecks away from that food stamp line. Be considerate of people's feelings in terms of what you say, how you say it and to whom you say it.

I was on public assistance for nine long years. I put up with the humiliation and the total degradation of those uncaring, unkind people who tried at every turn of the bend to rob me of my individuality and my dreams.

I met each turn of that bend armed with my dream, my MONKEY WRENCH, and a good, strong support system. Thus strengthened, I decided to finish my degree. After fulfilling the residency requirement, I enrolled in the University of Rio Grande, graduated in 1986 with my Bachelor's Degree in Social Work, and earned a State of Ohio Social Worker's License. I then founded CASA, and started Child Abuse Safety Actions.

After a brief hiatus, I started graduate school at Ohio University in Athens, Ohio. I remained on public assistance throughout that period of my life. In 1990, I earned my Master's degree and finally laid one MONKEY to rest. I moved out of Gallia County, and called and told the Department of Human Services what they could do with their next month's welfare check. My new life began with a job and guess what it was? It was a social work position for the Athens County Department of Human Services. Now I tell you, nothing is sweeter than sweet revenge. Well, as the saying goes, *"Turn about is fair play."*

I was given the joy of meeting the same dream breakers - these same individuals who tried to defeat me and break my spirit. What a joy! Turn about is fair play. And of course, I couldn't let the chance go by. At the next regional staff meeting I seized the opportunity to sit next to the old agency's director, one of the MONKEYS who had made my life so miserable for nine years. I said to him, *"Well, hello. Remember me?"* He responded, *"Of course."* I continued, *"Do you remember what I told you?"* He answered, *"You talk so much, it's hard to tell."* *"Thank you,"* I acknowledged, *"Now pay attention and you might learn something. I used to be your client, now I'm your colleague. Be nice, be nice to people, because you never know who they'll turn out to be!"* I went from receiving ADC to receiving my M.Ed.

Ironically, my situation had come full circle. It was a long hard struggle to pull myself out of poverty, but I am living proof that ONE MONKEY DON'T STOP NO SHOW! - Not even if that MONKEY is the great and mighty Department of Human Services!

Editor's Comment - Aleta Mays has not only said it all, but also done most of it. Her story should empower and inspire readers who doubt their ability to raise themselves above the negative mental conditioning they are victimized by. Her story reinforces *No Place For Ego: Don't Get Bad Getting Good* from section one of this book.

Aleta, author of the book *One Monkey Don't Stop No Show*, may be contacted at P.O. Box 6, Albany, OH 45710, (614) 698-2443.

"I've began watching carefully with whom I associate. Now I seek out people who have goals, direction, integrity, character and emulate a positive image of excellence."

- Ilinda Reese -

Commenting on The Power of Association

Isn't it funny how you remember the things you learned as a child and they suddenly make sense? I remember hearing my dad and mom, Pastor Lawrence and Theresa Boone, emphasizing to me the significant impact my choice of associations would have on my life.

Their words of wisdom said you become like those you associate with. If you have high standards and they do not, either you will bring them up or they will bring you down. It is more likely that the latter will happen. I remember the familiar statement of the civil rights leader, Jesse Jackson who said, *"Your attitude will determine your altitude."* and an anonymous writer who said *"You cannot soar like an eagle if you are surrounded by turkeys."*

As previously mentioned, I did not accept my parents explanation of the power of association until recent years. I've began watching carefully with whom I associate. Now I seek out people who have goals, direction, integrity, character and emulate a positive image of excellence. I seek out people who provide a supportive atmosphere that promotes growth. Those you enjoy being around, not only for what you receive from the association but what you can give. These individuals have been previously referred to by society as the *"movers and shakers"* because they not only become emotional about their creative thoughts but they apply what works to make it happen.

Negative people are always ready to point out the realities of your dreams. They are experts at throwing cold water on your passions. If one is reaching outside of their little perceptual box, negative people will tell you things according to how they see it. After talking with them you feel like a deflated balloon; Just drained. Les Brown refers to them as *"the dream killers."* I have learned to limit my involvement with this group and to join allegiance with those that do not watch things happen but make things happen, like the members of Worth Sharing Communications.

An association with children is important to me. I recently attended a play called *"Into The Woods"*, a play about the mystical, magical fantasies of fairy tales. The magic of the evening began when my associate, Tina Stumps, playing the leading role, sang a whimsical, melodious song. As I listened I was awe struck by one line in the play that said, *"wishes are children."* After asking several individuals what they felt the play writer was trying to say, I concluded that the statement alluded to the life and energy of children. Their imagination and creativity allows them to be liberated, not limited. Just as children develop to maturity with encouragement and attention, so will your wishes and dreams. Children are impossibility seekers. The writer Langston Hughes said, *"If dreams die, life is like a broken bird that cannot fly."* Associating with children keeps the child alive in us and reminds us of the uniqueness in each of us to accomplish the impossible.

Understanding the power of association caused me to accept God to be the most important influence in my life. Now understanding completely how we become like who we spend time with, I seek my direction and empowering from him. *"Spiritual growth results from absorbing and digesting truth and putting it to practice in daily life"* as quoted by White Eagle in the book, *Acts of Faith*. When researching successful men and women, I regularly encountered one stabilizing, consistent undercurrent. Their belief in God as the foundation of wisdom. By allowing God to shape and mold my life, the revelations provide me with an unlimited capacity to enjoy life.

Bettina Flores stated, *"Successful people succeed because they learn from their failures."* Another writer said, *"Learn from others mistakes, you won't have time in one lifetime to make them all."* In my lifetime I made a few mistakes, quite a few. I appreciate the love, respect and support I've received from my parents, children (Tammy, Eric and Raffael), and my associates, that influences my life and allows me to grow. Someone once said, *"If you see a turtle on the top of a fence post, know that he didn't get there by himself. He had help."* The **Prior Report Newsletter** stated, *"The success that you will attain is greatly influenced by the people with whom you associate."* Thank you for your associations.

To the author of this great work, Henry Ford, thank you for the opportunity and the power of your association.

Author's Comment - Candor, education and humor characterize a day with Ilinda. A powerful speaker and excellent seminar leader and workshop presenter, Ilinda refuses to let *dull or boring* enter her presentations. Always good for a surprise that leads directly to the truth, Ilinda has presented to business and industry and to numerous schools, civic organizations and churches.

Ilinda may be contacted at -

3851 East 177th St.
Cleveland, OH 44128
(216) 890-4121

"Our rightful place is where our consciousness has brought us, our truthful place is where our consciousness can take us."

- Patricia Wingard Carson -

Divine Order of Association

Knowing that the immutable laws of the universe are exact in their out-workings, we must strive to create the most intimate and the most powerful association any human being can attain. We must build a personal association (relationship) with our higher self and gain personal knowledge of the spiritual principles that govern our existence. Just as the galaxies are governed by the universal law of divine order, so are we as inhabitants of the universe. It is essential that we understand that order and apply the principles to our everyday lives.

Sometimes we allow ourselves to get so overly consumed with that which we can see with our physical eyes, that we neglect the gift of spiritual insight we each have been given. It is through this type of gross spiritual neglect that we subconsciously create animosities, disappointments, resentments, and continue to move from one toxic relationship to another. We fail to prepare ourselves to attract the association of higher energy into our world and affairs.

Within us lies the still and authoritative voice of our spiritual essence. The success of the horizontal relationships we have with mankind, hinges upon the solidarity of the vertical relationship we have with our Creator.

We can establish an intimate relationship with our higher self through prayer, physical fasting, mental fasting from negative thoughts, and meditation exercises that create inner peace and seek alignment with our purpose. This type of spiritual growth is as essential to our total-being as food, water, and sleep.

Once we take care of our spiritual, physical, and mental self, we inevitably create an energy field that attracts and binds us with powerful associations and experiences that are conducive to our purpose. The immutable laws of the universe will provide personal experiences for us that are in alignment with who we are, and will permit us to move from our rightful place into out truthful place. Our rightful place is where our consciousness has brought us, our truthful place is where our consciousness can take us.

Through life's trials, errors, and triumphs, I have learned that my associations are a direct reflection of my individual level of consciousness and not determined by some outside force. The strength of my relationships are as powerful as my consciousness believes them to be. The more intimate I become with my spirituality, the greater my outside experiences. And the degree to which I learn from my experiences, the higher my wisdom becomes. Thus, I'm able to walk in the light of knowing that I am magnificently made, wonderfully blessed, and powerfully endowed and great things happen through those who believe they can!

Author's Comment - WOW! Patricia Wingard Carson is the author of **Peculiar Pain**, ... *a close look at Black on Black sexual harassment and its impact.* Other published works include **Seeds of Greatness**: *The Power of the Imagination* and **The Secrets of Meditation**: *Tapping Into Your Intuitive Powers.*

Now I understand why State Senator Jeffrey Johnson said of Patricia's book **Peculiar Pain**, *"Not since the nation witnessed the story of Anita Hill and her experience at work with her supervisor, Clarence Thomas, has a story been told that clearly and dramatically exposes sexual harassment in the workplace."*

Now I understand why Patricia Brown of the **Call and Post** read **Peculiar Pain** from cover to cover in one sitting. Ms. Brown goes on to explain that **Peculiar Pain** is about *"How to deal with sexual harassment but it is also about self development and personal growth. "*

Patricia is the founder of Motivational Institute, Inc., a Human Resource Development firm in Columbus, Ohio. Married to former FBI agent Jeffrey Carson, she and Jeffrey are the proud parents of three sons, Dorian, Derrick and Christopher. Patricia is also the founder of Sexual Harassment and Education Month.

For information, contact Patricia at

Motivational Institute, Inc.
P.O. Box 328712
Columbus, OH 43232
Phone (614) 276-5155
Fax   (614) 274-7773

In Conclusion

Do you feel the power? Didn't it feel good to read and absorb positive information? Wasn't it rewarding during those moments to be unburdened by negative mental conditioning? If you devoted more time and effort to improving you and your surroundings, how much more power and purpose would you have? What obstacles could you overcome? What rewards would you enjoy? To achieve the greatness that is within us, we must answer these questions continuously.

One hundred and twenty-five pages ago you embarked on a journey. That journey has taken you into the minds and hearts of twelve highly motivated individuals. From different experiences and perceptions, they shared many ideas about challenge, growth, success, and personal and professional relationships.

The common current that exists in this ocean of uniqueness is that each of us has individual power and purpose. The belief shared among the writers is that operating alone we can make a ripple, but together we can make waves. This book could only have been written with the belief and effort of others.

It was several wide-eyed fifth grade students whose smiles and thank you letters caused me to understand the real issue. Thanks for the expectations and honesty of children.

It was a faithful and diligent wife who looked at one passage and replied, *"Do you really want to write it this way?"* Thanks for the reasoning power of someone not influenced by the emotion of the moment.

It was a very busy speaker, on the road seven days a week, who said *"Sure, I'll write a story to help out."* He called long distance from his car phone. He didn't need the exposure this book offered, although I believe he will benefit from it. Thanks for those who are willing to reach down the ladder.

It was a teenager and her younger sister that corrected the order of names on pages eighty-seven through ninety after I THOUGHT I put them in alphabetical order. They did the same with the Index. Then, they said with forgiving diplomacy, *"Oh, it was just a couple of mistakes."* Thanks for the power of young eyes and open minds. Thanks for the compassion of kind hearts.

It was God who made all these resources available to me. You have resources available to you. In your life there are or can be people and events ready to come into your dream and make it a reality. *The Power of Association* is constantly in motion, seeking people to enable, to energize, to catapult to greatness. Don't let your dream take place without you. The momentum and power of the universe can use you, but it will not wait for you.

As you face the challenges of life, harness, become a part of, and use *The Power of Association*. In this book is the roadmap to take you around life's roadblocks. Within these stories is the vision to turn life's stumbling blocks into stepping stones.

This book is a reminder that the power and purpose of one, enhanced, multiplied and compounded, is enough to overcome most of the challenges we face. My challenge and my reward is to be a part of your growth, to be counted as a positive force and inspiration in your life. Only God could have caused my thoughts and experiences to be connected to your life through *The Power of Association*. Use this book wisely and to paraphrase Maya Angelou, you'll rise, you'll rise, you'll rise.

Recommended Reading

Alston, Harvey. *Best The Best*. Dubuque, Iowa: Kendall/Hunt Publishing Company, 1995

Brown, Les. *Live Your Dreams*. New York: William Morrow and Company, 1992

Covey, Stephen. *7 Habits of Highly Effective People*. New York: Simon & Schuster, 1989

Ford, Henry. *Success Is You*. Dubuque, Iowa: Kendall/Hunt Publishing Company, 1995

Fraser, George. *Success Runs In Our Race*. New York: William Morrow and Company, 1994

Lawson, Dr. Robert L. *Destined For Greatness*. Dubuque, Iowa: Kendall/Hunt Publishing Company, 1994

Lewis, Lucius. *A Better Way of Taking Care of You*. Cleveland, Ohio: A.J. Lewis & Associates, 1994

Luks, Allan. *The Healing Power of Doing Good*. New York: Fawcett Columbine, 1996

Mackay, Harvey. *Swim With The Sharks*. New York: William Morrow and Company, 1988

Mays, Aleta. *One Monkey Don't Stop No Show*. Dubuque, Iowa: Kendall/Hunt Publishing Company, 1996

Robbins, Anthony. *Giant Steps*. New York: Simon & Schuster, 1994

Works Cited

Alston, Harvey. *Best The Best*. Dubuque, Iowa: Kendall/Hunt Publishing Company, 1995

Bemley, Dr. Jesse L. and Shiree L. *Bonding For Excellence*. Washington, DC: BDPA National, 1990

Bemley, Dr. Jesse L. and Shiree L. *Ideas In The Making*. Washington, DC: BDPA National, 1989

Caris-McManus, Jeannemarie. *A Conversation With Michael Gerber*. Cleveland, Ohio: COSE, May, 1994

Covey, Stephen. *7 Habits of Highly Effective People*. New York: Simon & Schuster, 1989

Ford, Henry. *Success Is You*. Dubuque, Iowa: Kendall/Hunt Publishing Company, 1995

Fraser, George. *Success Runs In Our Race*. New York: William Morrow and Company, 1994

King, Beverly. *Reflections*. Detroit, 1994

King Jr., Dr. Martin Luther. *Where Do We Go From Here?* New York: Harper & Row, 1968

Lewis, Lucius. *A Better Way of Taking Care of You*. Cleveland, Ohio: A.J. Lewis & Associates, 1994

Stella, Phillip J. *Marketing*. Cleveland, Ohio: COSE, May, 1994

Wilson, Vivian. *Get On Board!* Cleveland, Ohio: Data News, BDPA Cleveland, Summer, 1990

Reader and Audience Comments

"It has been said by many who attend yearly that this one was the best ever."

> Z. Ann Hoyle, President
> Hickory, North Carolina Branch - NAACP
> May, 1989

"Your speech should be published and made standard reading for teachers and PTA units."

> Dr. Jack Hearns, Superintendent
> Warrensville Hts., Ohio City Schools
> March, 1990

"Mr. Ford, they will not soon forget you."

> Ron Sobel, Acting President
> Cuyahoga Community College - Cleveland, Ohio
> May, 1991

"I want our speaker to know that the pulpit is open at Grace Missionary."

> Rev. Walter L. Boykins
> Grace Missionary Baptist Church
> July, 1992

"His voice is deep and velvety, his style methodical and deliberate. His strong, clear delivery emphasizes his faith in his message."

> Twinsburg, Ohio *Sun Times*
> May 23, 1993

Index

About The Author

Henry Ford's unique combination of attitude, persistence and faith is reflected in his speeches, workshops and writings. His second career as a speaker and writer is a success story that inspires hope and generates a call to action.

Despite aptitude tests that told him he could not, the author has astounded family, friends and acquaintances by his accomplishments. His extensive training and involvement in numerous organizations substantiate his belief in *The Power of Association*.

The author is a member of the Ohio Speakers Forum, the National Speakers Association, Toastmasters International, The Dream Team, Worth Sharing Communications, the Cleveland Business Consortium, the Black Data Processing Associates and the National Association of Investors Corporation.

A Magna Cum Laude graduate of Capital University's Adult Degree Program, Henry earned a degree in Business & Communications. His strong belief in continuing education is apparent by his constant attendance at seminars and workshops of noted trainers and others. He is a graduate of the Les Brown *Speaking For A Living Workshop*.

Mentored by noted professionals in the field of motivation such as Harvey Alston and Dr. Robert L. Lawson, Henry is acknowledged by some of the world's most respected speakers and authors. Noted speaker Les Brown on two occasions has publicly described Henry as *"a very powerful speaker."* Henry has also earned the public praise of businessman and speaker George Fraser, author of *Success Runs In Our Race*.

Need A Speaker?
Of Course You Do!

For a list of reasons too lengthy to mention, people today need the words of encouragement and empowerment. Whatever the occasion, if you are charged with the responsibility of motivating, training or entertaining students, employees, organization members, family member or others, I can help.

Let me bring you the knowledge, experience, commitment and purpose of not one, but many speakers, trainers and authors. As many speakers do, I offer you my services, but as few do, I offer you the benefits of synergism, the synergism of positive association.

If I am unable to satisfy your requirements because of schedule conflicts or other reasons, I will refer you to another speaker at no cost to you. We are committed to your satisfaction.

As a member of the *Ohio Speakers Forum*, the *National Speakers Association*, *The Dream Team* and *Worth Sharing Communications*, I am connected to some of the most powerful speakers and trainers in the world.

Contact me today so that we can discuss your needs and how I can be of service to you.

Henry Ford
"The Communicator"
P.O. Box 393
Twinsburg, OH 44087-0393
(216) 425-8776

Note: Area Code Change to 330 is being considered

Product Descriptions

Tapes, Booklets, T-Shirts and Other Products
See the following pages to order
Success Is You or *The Power of Association*

Booklets -

Affirmative Action: It's You - 47 page booklet designed to help you focus upon the fallacy and temporary nature of affirmative action, and to create your own affirmative action plan.

Publishing For Success - 12 page booklet designed to encourage the speaker to take the journey from speaking to writing. This booklet was used by the author for training at the Ohio Speakers Forum, a chapter of the National Speakers Association.

Audio Cassettes -

Affirmative Action Tape - 60 minute tape that will stimulate, educate and entertain. Includes the popular affirmative action speech delivered to the FORD-BRYSON, HANSIE SOLOMON Family Reunion in Atlanta, Georgia. Also contains comments from live radio talk shows and other motivational speeches.

Ready For Takeoff & More - 60 minute tape to entertain and delight you. Includes the popular *Ready For Takeoff* and other speeches.

The Latest Products & Services - As a part of our continual growth, we are constantly adding books, tapes, T-shirts and other products and services. Please contact us for descriptions of our latest offerings.

Order Form

Tapes, Booklets and Other Products

See the following pages to order
Success Is You or *The Power of Association*

YES! I want _____ copies of the booklet *Affirmative Action* at $ 4.95 each, plus $ 1.00 shipping and handling per book.

YES! I want _____ copies of the booklet *Publishing For Success* at $ 1.95 each, plus $ 1.00 shipping and handling per book.

YES! I want _____ copies of the audio cassette *Affirmative Action* at $ 4.95 each, plus $ 1.00 shipping and handling per tape.

YES! I want _____ copies of the audio cassette *Ready For Takeoff* at $ 4.95 each, plus $ 1.00 shipping and handling per tape.

Name _____

Phone (_____) _____

Address _____

City/State/Zip _____

Ohio residents add 6 1/4% State Sales Tax
Please make check or money order for total, payable to:

FORD & Associates

P.O. Box 393 - Twinsburg, OH 44087-0393
(216) 425-8776

Note: Area Code Change to 330 is being considered

Order Form

Success Is You

YES! I want _____ copies of *Success Is You* at $ 16.95 each, plus $ 3.50 shipping and handling per book. ISBN # 0-7872-0232-0.

Call 1-800-228-0810 to order by telephone or Fax 1-800-772-9165. Prepayment is required.

Name _____

Phone (_____) _____

Address _____

_____

City/State/Zip _____

Please make check payable to:

Kendall/Hunt Publishing Company

4050 Westmark Drive
Dubuque, Iowa 52004-1840

Order Form
The Power of Association

YES! I want _____ copies of *The Power of Association* at $16.95 each, plus $ 3.50 shipping and handling per book. ISBN # 0-7872-1789-1

Call 1-800-228-0810 to order by telephone or Fax 1-800-772-9165. Prepayment is required.

Name _____

Phone (_____) _____

Address _____

_____

City/State/Zip _____

Please make check payable to:

Kendall/Hunt Publishing Company
4050 Westmark Drive
Dubuque, Iowa 52004-1840